HURRICANES OVER MURMANSK

HURRICANES
OVER
MURMANSK

JOHN GOLLEY
Author of 'THE DAY OF THE TYPHOON'

First published in the UK in 1987
by Patrick Stephens Ltd

This edition published in 2001
by Airlife Publishing Ltd

British Library Cataloguing-in-Publication Data
  A catalogue record for this book
  is available from the British Library

ISBN 1 84037 298 2

Printed in England by St Edmundsbury Press Ltd, Bury St Edmunds, Suffolk

Airlife Publishing Ltd
101 Longden Road, Shrewsbury, SY3 9EB, England
E-mail: airlife@airlifebooks.com
Website: www.airlifebooks.com

Contents

Introduction

Flight Sergeant Charles 'Wag' Haw lay in his hammock swaying slightly with the roll of the aircraft carrier as it ploughed its way through calm waters towards the Arctic Circle. Close beside him in the cramped quarters, his chum and number two, Sergeant Pilot Ken 'Ibby' Waud had dozed off. In between the grinding and metallic banging noises made by the old carrier *Argus*, Wag could hear Ibby's snores and it made him laugh. Dear old Ibby, he thought, out to this world!

It was hot and stuffy down there and he couldn't switch himself off and get to sleep but lay staring at the ceiling which rocked slowly from side to side making him feel that he was suspended in mid-air — which indeed he was. His mind focused on the parties and piss-ups that he and Ibby had been on before they left Leconfield. Three times they had been sent on leave because the show had been postponed. It had become embarrassing to arrive back home in York having already said their goodbyes on the first two occasions. Turning up again had made them both feel uncomfortable and self-conscious so they took off for Scarborough and spent a hazy four days in a pub called 'The Old Bar'.

He had sometimes wondered how his father 'Fred' would have reacted had he told him that they were off to Russia. Fred had never liked him flying and was convinced that when war came he would be killed. His father wasn't alone in that respect because Wag himself felt likewise. That was one of the reasons why he hadn't married his girlfriend, May, to whom he had been engaged for over a year. There was absolutely no point in getting himself hitched up with a war on and he wanted his freedom to make the most of his life and devote himself to his one abiding passion which was flying. Being a realist, he accepted the fact that he would probably get the chop sometime but meanwhile life was bloody exciting and he was going to enjoy every minute of it.

Looking back over the past twelve months gave him a warm glow of satisfaction and self-confidence in coming through the Battle of Britain and opening his scoresheet. The actions had been savage and only lasted for a few minutes or even less but he was well aware that the odds weighed heavily against any fighter pilot coming through. Even thinking about it seemed to pump the adrenalin through his system and excite him. He could still picture layers of bombers hurtling towards him looming up larger and larger in his windscreen until he picked out the nearest one and in a split second had a go. It had always given him an overwhelming sensation of elation as he lined up his gunsight for the kill and then with wings vibrating from the recoil of his Browning machine-guns pumping out the lead he flashed past the bomber at frightening speed. Thinking back he realized that the moment of truth came when he had broken away from these head-on attacks. Suddenly he was one of the hunted feverishly screwing his head round searching the sky for Messerschmitts. A tell-tale sparkle from the sun's rays bouncing off a fuselage had usually been the signal for him to perform gymnastics with his Hurricane, fighting for his life. Swinging slowly in the comfort of his hammock, he could see those Me 109s diving down on him and he remembered that those had been the occasions when he couldn't stop his leg twitching after he had landed and got out of his aircraft. He recalled telling one of the chums that he had had 'a touch of the knee trembles'.

It had bothered him a little at first but he got used to it, putting it down to a normal reflex action after the tension of a scrap. He had told his friend Ibby on several occasions that aerial combat, as far as he was concerned, was a capsule of excitement which gripped him and he had no feelings once the action started.

Lying there he found it almost impossible to believe that they were really on their way to Russia. Ever since leaving Scapa Flow everything had been shrouded in mist and they had seen nothing except white foam rushing alongside. It was like being in cloud all the time. He had often watched a naval chap who was always up front at the sharp end looking down and keeping his eyes riveted on some kind of floating drogue towed by the lead ship in front. The drogue bumped up and down sending out two white V-shaped spumes of foam. Somebody always kept watch on this drogue which seemed to provide the only means for the carrier to keep station in the convoy. Life in the old *Argus* was like living in a cocoon totally removed from reality.

They seemed to have been at sea for some time now and he worked out that today must be the last day of August. Life on board, he considered, wasn't too bad although a trifle boring. A daily Naval Commanding Officer's inspection of quarters and a few official talks but little else. The grub was very good and the rum ration highly acceptable, but he missed his flying.

Sometimes, he would go and take a look at his machine down below the flight deck and sit in the cockpit. He loved the smell of his new aeroplane which was only a fuselage because the wings still had to be assembled. It gave him a rather special feeling of togetherness adjusting the seat and getting a feel of the controls. The day, he thought, would soon be coming when his machine would be ready for flying and going up to the flight deck.

All the Squadron Hurricanes were brand new Mark IIBs armed with twelve Browning machine-guns each but the pilots had never flown them. He and Ibby had joked about the fact that their first flight in their new machines would be somewhat hairy. It certainly was going to kick off that way, he thought, because none of them had taken off from a carrier before. At least it was going to be a new experience and it would certainly make a novel entry in his log book. He could see himself writing in the duty column, 'took off from aircraft carrier *Argus* and landed in Russia'. He recalled Ibby saying that all they had to do after they staggered off the carrier and joined Squadron formation was to find an obscure Russian airfield somewhere inside the Arctic coast about fifteen miles from a place called Murmansk. They had both laughed at the time — but it was no joke.

He felt the ship altering course by the change in the swing of his hammock. Ibby was still dead to the world and he wondered momentarily where they were. Probably somewhere off Iceland in the Arctic seas way north of the Norwegian coast he concluded. All he knew was they they were going to keep well away from Norway where the Germans had airfields and naval bases. Thinking about Germans reminded him that the war was going badly for the Russians. He had heard it on the news and it sounded as if the Krauts were doing in Russia what they did in the Low Countries in 1940. It was the way in which radio announcers were talking about heroic defensive battles when it was obvious to everybody that the Russians were retreating on all fronts. If the worst happened and the Russians caved in then he thought 151 Wing would be in a bloody marvellous position stuck up there on the northernmost tip of the Arctic coast.

The chums never discussed it because everybody believed that the Navy or the RAF would get them out. There was no future in talking about it, anyway, because the new Wing had been posted to Russia and that was all there was to it. Not that either he or Ibby worried. They were looking forward to some action. There hadn't been much of that since the Battle of Britain except convoy patrols which in the main had been dead boring.

The throbbing of the engines rumbled on and he could feel himself getting drowsy at last. The thought of climbing into that new Mark II Hurricane with its twelve guns brought him out of his comatose state making him appreciate how keen he was to get back into the air for a scrap. All the others were the same, especially Ibby. Old Ibby had so far missed all the action through no fault of his own and he was mad keen to catch up with the others. He was bloody lucky to have Ibby as his number two. Ibby would never let him down.

The idea of meeting Russian fighter pilots fascinated him. He visualized them as rough and tough 'down the hatch' vodka types. A bit crude, perhaps, but good chaps for all that. He had no idea what the airfield would be like or the Russian landscape. It was late summer in Russia but he thought that there was bound to be some snow around because they would be so far north. Pictures of forests, lakes, Cossacks, peasants and little villages flashed through his mind. The airfield was called Vianga and somebody had told him that there was a village just outside so there should be a chance for a few piss-ups, he thought. Anyway, in a few days they were all going to find out — and he couldn't wait.

*   *   *

Few people are aware that the RAF sent a Hurricane Wing to Russia in 1941. The newspapers picked it up at the time and printed photographs of the Wing in action but there is little, if anything, in the history books recording the expedition. During the short period during which the Wing was in action before the winter closed in, British fighter pilots shot down fifteen German aircraft for the loss of one Hurricane. On escort duties when their Hurricanes provided cover for Russian light bombers not one bomber was lost. Apart from proving the capabilities of the Hurricane fighter in action, the Wing taught the Russians how to fly and to service and erect Hurricane aircraft, which was the most important function of the project.

In the broad perspective of RAF history the 151 Wing operation in North Russia was a tiny fragment — a small side show involving some 550 officers and men and fifty pilots. But there were deeper implications. During July 1941 the Russians were retreating an all fronts and it looked as if Hitler's dream of a lightning victory might well be within his grasp. Premier Stalin was making impossible demands on the Allies and wanted Britain to open up a second front in Europe immediately and set in motion a massive aid programme covering all fields of military equipment, supplies and raw materials.

Fighter aircraft were high on the list of priorities and Winston Churchill made arrangements to send 200 fighters including some Hurricanes as soon as possible. On 21 July 1941, he telegraphed Stalin and told him that he was considering basing some British fighter squadrons on Murmansk. Churchill didn't waste any time and when Air Marshal Portal handed him a plan he ordered him to go right ahead. 151 Wing, comprising two squadrons, Nos 81 and 134, was formed in the last few days of July and ordered to get ready to embark for Russia.

There was very little that Churchill could do immediately to help Stalin stem the tide of the German advance. The war was of titanic proportions and substantial aid which could only come from America would take time to put into effect. Churchill was then under severe pressure from Stalin and it needed something more than promises and forecasts of aid to come to reassure the Russian leader that the British heart was in the right place.

His gesture to despatch a British Fighter Wing to Murmansk obviously had little military significance in the grand strategy, and history records that much later Churchill regretted that he hadn't sent ten or even twelve squadrons. But, however small, the Expedition had great public relations value when good will between the two countries was at a premium. For example, there are only four Englishmen who have been awarded the Order of Lenin and they were all members of 151 Wing: the station commander, Wing Commander Ramsbottom Isherwood, the two squadron commanders, Squadron Leaders Tony Rook and Tony

Miller, and Flight Sergeant Wag Haw, who was the top scoring fighter pilot in North Russia.

In writing this book I have set the story of 151 Wing in North Russia against the traumatic events of those times both from a military and political point of view. It is an exciting adventure story from the moment that the Wing arrived at Vianga when 'Operation Barbarossa' — the code name for the German invasion of Russia — was within striking distance of achieving a successful conclusion. German General Dietl's 'Mountain Corps' was only a few miles from Murmansk and savage fighting was going on among the labyrinth of lakes and pools of swamp surrounding the town. The Luftwaffe were bombing the airfield and the German push to capture the port had reached a crescendo.

Hurricane pilots, many of whom had fought in the Battle of Britain, were soon scrambled to fight the familiar Messerschmitts, Heinkels, Dorniers and Junkers 88s, but in very different circumstances and battle conditions. A few weeks later the first snow fell on Murmansk and the Arctic winter began to descend. After handing all their aeroplanes, gear and equipment over to the Russians, they were told that they would be evacuated by train on a long and tortuous route through Russia down towards the Crimea. But the news came through that the Germans had advanced and cut the rail links making it impossible for them to move out over land.

Daylight diminished until it became a half-lidded affair lasting only about two hours. Arctic gales swept across the sixty miles of barren tundra landscape surrounding Murmansk turning it into an ice-packed desert with nothing but rock and scree. The German advance towards Murmansk had been blast frozen in its tracks and life for Germans and Russians alike was becoming a battle for human survival. There was nothing that the Expedition could do but sit it out and wait for the Navy. Fortunately for them the port of Murmansk remained open all year, thanks to the Gulf Stream.

The names of the ports of Murmansk and Archangel are indelibly imprinted on the minds of all those naval and merchant seamen whose convoys carrying aid for the Soviet Union ran the gauntlet across the Barents Sea. The 151 Wing Expedition was a fragment of that aid programme and was carried in one of the earliest convoys to make the trip. At that time aid was just beginning to trickle into the two ports and during the whole of 1941 only eight convoys set sail for Russia. This trickle soon turned into a torrent as aid from America and Britain reached full flood.

These ports, therefore, and Murmansk in particular during the depths of winter, played a vital role in the German/Russian war. Aid to Russia was part of the Expedition story and I have included some of the dialogue between Churchill, Stalin and Roosevelt which took place in the latter half of 1941 when the leaders were formulating a gigantic programme.

The theme throughout the book is naturally the story of the Wing and the pilots in particular. The main character is Charles 'Wag' Haw who received the Order of Lenin in Russia and was awarded the Distinguished Flying Medal upon his return home. Shortly afterwards he was commissioned and went on to win the Distinguished Flying Cross, surviving four tours of operations and becoming a Wing Commander. 'Wag', as he was known throughout the RAF, lived in York, joined the RAFVR in 1939 and did his early training at Brough. Several of his associates, who went with 81 Squadron to Russia, came from York and its surrounds and our story begins in York when Wag was struggling hard to become an RAF pilot.

Chapter 1
York — pre-war

Young Haw, like many others who joined the RAF, had his first flight when Alan Cobham's flying circus arrived on Rawcliffe field on the outskirts of York. He was ten years old at the time and his father, with some misgivings, gave him five shillings for his first flight so that he could join his friend Malcolm Gray who lived a few doors down the road. The boys were helped into an old radial-engined biplane — an Avro 504 with a skid between its front wheels — and had a fifteen-minute flip round the city. The youngsters were captivated by their adventure and both of them were determined to become pilots one day.

Haw had been christened Charlton in deference to a wealthy old Aunt Charlton who lived in Didsbury outside Manchester. His family had hopes for an inheritance and even named their house 'Didsbury' as a further mark of their respect. Unfortunately, his aunt had other ideas and made no mention of Charlton or the family in her will. So young Haw started life as Charlton Haw living at Didsbury House, Fifth Avenue, Old York.

His father had called him Charlie from the outset and the lad was glad that he did because the name Charlton sounded a bit posh and would have made life a trifle difficult for him in the little Yorkshire council school, Tang Hall, on the local estate. Young Haw inherited his father's aptitude for anything mechanical and as a boy spent most of his money acquiring stocks of Meccano. He and his friend, Malcolm Gray, pooled their resources and won several prizes sponsored by Meccano in Liverpool including one for building a giant car and another for making a wireless detector van in 1935. Getting absorbed with anything mechanical was only one of his interests because he learned to play the piano from the age of eight and began to acquire a good ear for music.

One evening his father surprised him by suddenly offering to send him to the local grammar school, Archbishop Holgate's, in York, pointing out that his friend Malcolm went there. Charlie didn't want to go and said that he was happy at Tang Hall. He liked the school and it suited him. He couldn't see any advantage or reason why he should change. Apart from that the thought of going to another school made him nervous and he always felt shy when meeting new people, not knowing what to say.

In his mid-teens, Charlie started work as an apprenticed lithographer at William Sessions and Company of New Earswick a few miles from the city. His bosses were Quakers and rather strict but he did well in the business and at the age of seventeen he was put in charge of the new offset litho machine churning out 3,000 copies an hour until the union official stepped in to put a brake on his enthusiasm. During that time, his father bought him a motor cycle and life began to open up.

Charlie Haw and three chums formed a group including saxophone, bass, drums and piano and they toured village halls, being paid five bob each for a nightly performance. This was big money for Charlie who was then only earning seventeen-and-six a week with Sessions. He was soon able to trade in his old motor cycle and with his father's help buy a brand new 350 cc Ariel to which he attached a copper pipe to make a more splendid noise.

After a late Saturday night playing with the group, Charlie used to get up at 5.00 am to shoot off to Rowntrees Park for tennis and then go to pick up his girlfriend, May. But despite all these activities his one overriding ambition in life was to join the RAF and become a fighter pilot. He would watch any flying film several times over and when he had seen *Hell's Angels* every night during one week the cinema usherette shone her torch on him and said, 'Not you again!'

He was determined to get into the RAF somehow but he hadn't the faintest idea how to go about it. There were no advertisements in those days telling people how and where they could volunteer and the whole thing was a mystery to him. One summer evening in 1938 his chum Malcolm Gray came to the house and told him how he could volunteer for pilot training with the RAFVR. 'You will have to go to Hull for an interview and a medical', Malcolm said, 'I'll give you the address. As a matter of fact, I've already been accepted, you know.' That was enough for Charlie and he shot off the following day to try his luck.

The excursion didn't go as well as he had hoped. He was told that he had a lazy eye and also needed further education before they would accept him. The doctor said that he should be able to strengthen the muscles of his lazy eye by exercising it. This he could do by staring at a pencil and moving it slowly at arm's length towards the tip of his nose. But it was made clear by his interviewer that it was entirely up to him to do something about his level of education. The first thing he did was to enrol for evening classes on three nights a week at the Leeds College of Technology. He was well aware, from his interview, that he needed to improve his mathematics, English and general knowledge and he wasn't going to let any such problem stand in his way.

Life became very hectic for Charlie during the following months what with his job, travelling to Leeds for his studies, playing the piano with the group and finding time for his girlfriend. His family used to laugh at him sometimes, seeing him sitting in a corner going cross-eyed over his pencil — which he did with monotonous regularity. But they were also worried about him and this flying business. His mother, Cissie, who had been an invalid for several years, put on a brave face and encouraged him, but deep down inside she was frightened of young Charlie getting himself killed. Charlie was someone very special for her because he had arrived somewhat accidentally some ten years after his brother Fred was born.

In February 1939, Charlie was passed by the RAF Selection Board in Leeds and kitted out as a Sergeant in the RAFVR. He was to be paid a retaining fee of forty pounds per annum plus ten shillings a day Sergeant Pilot's expenses whenever he went flying at weekends. He could scarcely believe his luck. He would be making as much money in one day from his flying and piano playing as he did in a week working his litho machine at Sessions. To be actually paid to go flying, he thought, was a fantastic achievement and he couldn't help indulging in a little self-congratulation. He had wanted to be a pilot more than anything else in the world and now he had the chance of becoming one. It sounded too good to be true and he could hardly wait to get up in the air. They told him in Hull that he would have to do more studying and be required to pass a written examination before he got his wings. Three lectures a week in Hull, they said, and he would do his elementary training on Blackburn B2s at Brough airfield on the banks of the River Humber.

Three weeks later, on a Saturday morning in early March 1939, Charlie drove his 350cc Ariel through the gates of Brough airfield. He was keyed up with excitement, lapping up the atmosphere around him like a puppy being taken for his first walk in the country where everything was new and mysterious. Peering round an open hangar door he gaped at the silver machines inside and sniffed for the first time the pungent smell of aeroplanes, a stale aroma of petrol, dope and oil which lingers in the nostrils.

He stood there entranced, a slightly shortish young man with strong shoulders and legs, small roundish face with pointed chin, dark vital hair and blue eyes. That moment when eighteen-year-old Charlie Haw savoured the close proximity of aeroplanes was to become the turning point of his life for many years to come. His strong and compact build, agile mind, aggressive spirit and sensitive hands were qualities which were going to stand him in good stead as a fighter pilot. Having learned to play the piano from an early age gave him a high degree of feeling in his fingertips and also enabled him to co-ordinate mind and body without having to think about it.

The weather was set fair for flying on that Saturday morning when Charlie, dressed in a white boiler suit and carrying his helmet, went outside to meet his instructor. He could see people gathered in little groups standing around the perimeter of the airfield staring at the silver biplanes as they were being wheeled out of the hangars. They made him feel important as he strode up to his instructor and introduced himself in his soft-spoken broad Yorkshire accent. The great man, who was a retired Flying Officer from the RAF, nodded and told him to get into the Blackburn B2 marked *G-ACES* and wait for him.

Charlie's first flight convinced him beyond any shadow of doubt that he was lucky enough to be completely at home in the air. He sat beside his instructor and listened intently, getting the feel of the aircraft through the movement of the controls. After a few trips, when he had completed two hours' flying, his instructor flicked the B2 upside down while making a circuit of the airfield and told Charlie to take over and roll out the machine to the upright position on the crosswind leg before turning in on the approach. This manoeuvre required a lot of nerve and confidence because the aircraft was relatively close to the ground and all the controls were reversed when the machine was inverted. But Charlie enjoyed it.

Flying was a challenge and he was determined to do better in the air then anyone else.

One Saturday evening about seven o'clock the flight commander, Flight Lieutenant Snelling, came up to him and said, 'Get into *G-ACES* and start the fan going, old boy. Off you go and play'. Snelling was a rather 'wizard prang' type and this was his way of sending Charlie off solo. Going solo for the first time is always a big moment in any pilot's life but for young Haw it was a double achievement. He had only had a mere four hours and twenty minutes of dual instruction. Nine hours dual was reckoned to be very good for any pilot, and some took eleven or twelve hours before being sent off on their own.

Going solo when he did put Charlie way ahead of his contemporaries and he was proud of it. He had always called his instructor 'Sir' as a mark of respect and the two men got on very well together. The experienced ex-RAF Flying Officer had realized that he had a natural pilot in Charlie Haw and gave him his head. It wasn't long before Charlie was up there on his own performing aerobatics over his home in Fifth Avenue, Old York. This created quite a local stir in those days when flying was a novelty and generally regarded as a rich man's pastime.

During this period he sold his 350cc Ariel and bought a four-wheel BSA Scout — an acquisition which gave him a bit of upmanship with the fraternity at Brough where the atmosphere was that of a select flying club. His boyhood friend Malcolm Gray was there and Ibby Waud who also came from York. Both chaps had been to Archbishop Holgate's Grammar School and Ibby worked for his father who was an accountant. Malcolm and Ibby, however, were several months ahead of him on the course and were flying Hawker Harts — a front line aircraft in those days.

Charlie thought that he must have been doing well on the course when his instructor allowed him to fly a Hawker Hart while the rest of his associates were still on Blackburn B2s. Sitting in that elegant and powerful machine he couldn't help thinking how lucky he was. He found it hard to believe that he, a machine operator and coming from a council school, should have had the opportunity to fly a real combat aircraft.

He couldn't help looking at life that way. Everything that absorbed his interest had been a challenge and flying was the biggest one of his life. He just had to do it better than anybody else and at Brough he knew damn well from the few flying hours he had 'put in' that he had sublime confidence in his ability to control an aircraft. Performing those upside down circuits had given him something which he instinctively felt would stand him in good stead if war came. Everybody at Brough realized that if that happened then they would all be part of it.

*　　*　　*

Shortly after Charlie Haw had done his first solo flight, Adolf Hitler, contrary to the Munich 'agreement', occupied the rest of Czechoslovakia. The date was 15 March 1939. The RAF had just emerged from the stagnation of the 'thirties and was in the process of re-equipping squadrons with modern fighters. Large numbers of Hurricanes and Spitfires had been delivered during the four months between February and May of that year and at long last the old biplanes including Bulldogs, Gauntlets, Furies, Harts and Demons were being phased out. With war staring Europe in the face the re-equipment programme for Fighter Command was accelerated. It had needed to be because only a few months previously, in late September 1938, there were only six squadrons of the RAF equipped with modern eight-gun fighters. These consisted of one Spitfire squadron and five Hurricane squadrons none of which were fully operational. In July 1939, less than three months before war was declared, the Air Marshals at last began to evaluate the effects that a German invasion of the Low Countries would have on Fighter Command.

*　　*　　*

While the Air Council was discussing the future strength and commitments of Fighter Command in a European war situation, Charlie Haw and his associates were carrying on with their flying programmes. Flying and having fun were the only things that mattered as far as they were concerned. Their ultimate goal was to get their wings and a posting to an auxiliary fighter squadron. Charlie, determined to 'get in' as many hours as possible, spent his two-week holiday flying from Brough. He had become engaged to May, who cheerfully accepted the fact that she was destined to play second fiddle to an aeroplane. Everything was going well for Charlie. Apart from flying, which was his first love, he was becoming quite a wealthy young man. The ten bob a day Sergeant Pilot's allowance, his RAFVR retaining fee of forty pounds a year plus extra cash from his piano playing and his weekly salary of seventeen shillings and sixpence allowed him to run his motor car and have money to spare.

Apart from weekend flying, he still had to attend three lectures a week in Hull so May didn't see much of him. They did, however, manage to get away for a few days just before the Munich crisis. It was in late August and they stayed in an old converted railway carriage on the east coast which the family used as a holiday retreat. Both of them knew in their hearts that there was a good chance of war breaking out and they discussed the question of getting married. Charlie wouldn't go ahead with the idea saying that he would probably be killed flying during the war and it was wrong for either of them to get hitched up. This hadn't been an excuse on his part for avoiding the issue. He really believed that the chances of survival for any fighter pilot in aerial warfare were negligible. Films and books about First World War pilots in action on the Western Front had made this abundantly clear.

A few days later on 1 September Charlie received his call-up papers and was told to report to No 4 Initial Training Wing at Bexhill-on-Sea. The news that Great Britain was at war with Germany came on 3 September when the Prime Minister, Neville Chamberlain, delivered his radio broadcast. The outbreak of war was to fulfil young Haw's lifelong ambition of becoming an RAF fighter pilot. He had long since appreciated that there hadn't been the remotest chance of getting himself into the regular Air Force and that he had been damned lucky to have made the RAFVR.

Now, the war had changed everything and he was going to grab his opportunities. Learning to fly had been an exhilarating and satisfying experience. He always enjoyed the feel and sensual pleasure of controlling an aircraft in flight but there was far more to it than that. Flying had given him a new dimension in life which he found difficult to put into words. He hadn't been able to talk to anybody about it, not even his family or his girlfriend. He had tried on several occasions over the past few weeks to have a chat with his father over a pint in the Conservative Club but it was hopeless. Dad didn't understand war because he had never been involved in it. During the 1914–18 show, as an electrical engineer, he had been in a reserved occupation.

It had made Charlie a little sad in a way because he loved his father and would have liked to talk to him about his great love of flying and his ultimate ambition to become a fighter pilot. Dad had always been kind and generous to him and the family had always been well provided for. Looking back, he remembered how proud he had been when his father had owned the first car in Fifth Avenue, which was quite something in those days. As a boy he used to help Dad strip it down, grease and polish it every Sunday morning. Thinking about it had made him realize that he had been spoilt throughout his life, probably because he was the baby of the family.

When his mother handed him an envelope marked OHMS she must have guessed what was inside, but she smiled, watching him bubbling over with excitement. Dear Cissie, unlike the others, never said anything about his flying but she must have worried about him. She had been an invalid then for several years and only been able to sit back and watch life pass her by. The family had known that war was imminent for some weeks for his brother-in-law, who was in the Territorial Army, had been called up and his sister Dot had moved in to look after them.

But it was quite a shock for them to see him go right at the outbreak of war, although Charlie was thrilled at the thought that he was actually going to be a fighter pilot in a war situation. The boys in the flying school at Brough talked about their hopes and aspirations and he recalled big Ibby Waud saying that it would be like a dream come true. Ibby had thought about it so much even before he started flying. He told the boys that he sometimes wondered if he hadn't been an SE.5 pilot in a previous life. He had visualized what a take-off, a loop and a roll would be like before he ever got into a aeroplane. And when he began training, he said, it was exactly as he thought it would be. It was a realization that it was right for him and that was what he should be doing.

Charlie had pricked up his ears when Ibby had mentioned that his father, who was an accountant, couldn't understand why he was interested in flying when he should have been more keen on the income tax act of 1925. Ibby said that he had always wanted to join the Air Force and even considered going off as a boy apprentice at the age of sixteen but decided against it because his sole ambition was to fly. He and his father often had words about it and in the end he told his father that he wasn't going to spend the rest of his life behind a bloody office desk and that was that.

The other chaps, who came from different walks of life, felt the same way. Civilian life had been a rather boring affair for most of them and playing about in their Blackburn B2s pretending to dogfight over the countryside surrounding Hull was a much more invigorating pastime. When Charlie received his call-up papers he found it almost impossible to believe that he could forget all about operating his litho machine at William Sessions and concentrate solely on flying. It seemed too good to be true. The thought of becoming a wartime fighter pilot excited him beyond measure. He already had eighty hours flying in his log book and was confident that he would soon get his wings and find himself on a fighter squadron. He could barely wait for that moment to come.

The RAF, however, was in no hurry to rush Charlie Haw or anybody else through his training despite the national emergency. There was no sense of urgency in Training Command at that time and peacetime attitudes prevailed. Even the outbreak of war had no effect upon policy and training programmes going through the system. Haw had to give up his flying and do an ITW course at Bexhill-on-Sea which included parades, square bashing, physical training and lectures. Ibby Waud and his chums were more fortunate because they were posted straight to an Advanced Flying Training School.

Ibby had been in the RAFVR for several months before Charlie had appeared on the scene and looked upon him as a little 'sprog'. Seniority and flying experience was all that mattered and Ibby admitted that he only spoke to Charlie because they both came from York and knew one another. 'I remember the poop, poop of his little motor cycle when he used to come in through the gates at Brough', he said, 'and we'd meet every now and again in a pub on our way back to York.'

The RAF has always been a Service fond of nicknames and Charlie Haw was no exception. His associates began to call him 'Wag' which was to stick with him throughout his Service life. This was hardly surprising because in Yorkshire, a Charlie is usually known as Wag. Apart from that there was a strip cartoon appearing in a local Sheffield paper entitled, 'Charlie Wagg — the boy burglar'. So Charlie became Wag Haw and will remain so throughout this book.

In late November 1939 Wag Haw was posted to No 5 Flying Training School at Sealand situated just off the North Wales coast a few miles from Chester. He was lucky because the FTS had just been re-equipped with the Miles Master Mark 1 and his course was the first one to be flying the new machine. The Master was an advanced gull wing trainer; a two-seater monoplane powered by a Rolls-Royce Kestrel XXX engine giving it maximum speed of 264 mph at 15,000 ft — a considerable performance at that time. Wag was lucky because the Miles Master was to be used as the basic trainer for those pilots destined to fly Hurricanes and Spitfires.

Features including a retractable undercarriage, split trailing edge flaps and an advanced cockpit layout made it an ideal machine for the job.

The course was to last nearly six months and most of it was conducted during the 'phoney' war — a period when the British Expeditionary Force was settling into Europe and a stalemate situation had developed along the front. It gave Fighter Command a 'heaven sent' opportunity to equip with modern fighters and train pilots — eight vital months to get on with its replacement programme without coming under pressure from enemy action.

When Wag Haw and Ibby Waud did their service flying training during late 1939 and early 1940 they were astonished to find that Training Command operated as if the war didn't exist. Courses were measured for efficiency in terms of weekly flying hours, regular peacetime routine was rigidly observed, and everything had to be authorized, approved and duly signed before any action could be taken. Although more training courses were being fed into the system, the national emergency still hadn't made any impact on the rigid structure of RAF Training Command. The war might have been a million miles away as far as the trainee pilots were concerned!

*   *   *

Wag Haw had already got his wings and was completing his advanced training course at Sealand when the phoney war erupted into bloody conflict. The German 'Blitzkrieg' machine began to roll through Belgium and across Northern France. For the first time the new Hurricanes and Spitfires came face to face with the Luftwaffe in prolonged aerial combat on a gigantic scale. Many pre-war theories and tactics employed by the RAF since World War 1 were torn apart during six weeks of non-stop combat.

The Luftwaffe, operating as the advanced striking force of Panzer divisions and mechanized infantry, displayed a new concept of the role of air power in battle. A strategy which co-ordinated air and ground forces in an attacking role and one which was to be successfully employed by the German High Command until the Russian winter of 1941 when the 'Blitzkrieg' machine became frozen to a standstill.

Over 450 British fighters were lost during the battle for France. The vast majority of these were Hurricanes, of which many were destroyed on the ground or had to be put out of action during the retreat. The first six days of combat had virtually decided the issue because basically there weren't enough fighter squadrons to neutralize Luftwaffe attacks and gain control of the air. There were some compensations for Fighter Command in that its modern fighters and pilots had performed well and had inflicted heavy losses on the enemy, but the balance sheet of gains and losses in the air was immaterial because the battle had been lost and France had fallen.

* * *

Ibby Waud, several months ahead of Wag Haw in seniority and flying experience, would have found himself fighting over France in the cockpit of a Hurricane if he hadn't been desperately unlucky. At the outbreak of war he had been posted to an Advanced Flying Training School equipped with Hawker Harts and naturally expected to find himself eventually posted to a fighter squadron. But much to his astonishment and disgust he was sent to Bomber Command to do a conversion course with a squadron flying Wellington bombers.

His boyhood dreams of becoming 'Biggles' shooting down lots of aircraft on the Western Front were shattered and he wondered how he was going to tell his father that he had ended up becoming a bomber pilot. But after he had completed his first circuit and bump in a Wimpey, his Flight commander took him and a number of others on one side and told them that they hadn't got enough night flying hours and posted them back to their previous Flying Training School to remedy the situation.

However, the chief flying instructor at Hullavington told him that it was impossible for them to give him night flying experience on his own and that he would have to join the next intake and do the course all over again. Ibby thought that the whole thing was ridiculous, particularly as some of the other chaps on his original course had already been posted to fighter squadrons. He found himself back where he had started and the thought of having to do another two months on Hawker Harts seemed to him a complete waste of time when all he had to do was to get some night flying hours under his belt.

Much to his delight when he had finished the course he was posted to No 3 Fighter Squadron who were flying Hurricanes from Kenley. He arrived at the beginning of May 1940 and was told to do some flying in the Squadron Miles Master before they would allow him up in a Hurricane. As the junior Sergeant Pilot he had to do duty pilot. This was in a wooden shack at the end of the runway and on the night of 9/10 May he was stuck out there in case an aircraft should suddenly appear and want to come in for a landing. It was usually a boring affair when nothing happened but at 4.30 am the telephone rang.

Somewhat bleary eyed he picked it up and said, 'Sergeant Waud, here'. He got quite a shock when an officious voice ordered him to wake up his commanding officer immediately and inform him that the Germans had invaded Belgium. No 3 Squadron were to be ready to take off for Merville in Northern France by midday.

After this dramatic news had sunk in, everybody was dashing about and in the general melee of that morning nobody paid any attention to Ibby and when the Squadron took off he was left standing at dispersals. Nothing was going to stop him from getting over to France so he surreptitiously clambered aboard a transport aircraft with the ground crews. Merville had been a famous First World War fighter station and the Squadron was soon scrambled to cover the retreat.

Ibby, full of enthusiasm, managed to confront his CO, Squadron Leader Gifford, who told him that he couldn't possibly stay with the Squadron. 'You haven't even flown a Hurricane yet, Waud', he said, 'I'm afraid that you'll have to go back to Kenley. I can't keep you here, I'm sorry.' The CO was right because No 3 Squadron was continuously in combat for the next ten days and suffered heavy casualties. The Squadron claimed to have shot down nine assorted aircraft in one day which gives some idea of the ferocity of the fighting as it covered the retreat which ended, finally, in the Dunkirk evacuation.

A frustrated and angry Ibby Waud returned to Kenley cursing his luck. He reckoned that he could have stepped straight out of a Hawker Hart and into a Hurricane and flown it without any trouble. It was too bloody bad, he thought, that he hadn't managed to fly the Hurricane before the Squadron moved out and he was mad and resentful about missing the action and being away from his Squadron.

When Kenley sent him to HQ Fighter Command for a posting it made matters worse. The Flight Lieutenant there said that he had nothing for him as far he could make out. Then, he said, 'Do me a favour Sergeant Waud. Pop down to Dengie Flats in Essex, it's just off Bradwell Bay. They need someone to look after the firing range for a couple of weeks. That'll give me time to find something for you.'

The fortnight passed but no posting came through for him. A strong, determined and highly intelligent character, he tried everything he knew to get himself out of that backwater and in so doing obviously made a nuisance of himself and ruffled a few feathers. But it was no good and the only thing he could do was to keep trying. The weeks turned into months and then the Battle of Britain started which made matters worse.

The fact that he was stuck on a bloody firing range when the country was fighting for its life and screaming out for fighter pilots was something he could stand no longer. He packed his bags without saying a word to anyone, left Dengie Flats and presented himself at HQ Fighter Command angry and disillusioned.

Having taken matters into his own hands, Ibby knew that he was in trouble and they threatened him with a court martial. Fortunately for him somebody took up his case and he found himself posted back to No 3 Squadron who were then at Wick, some three miles from John O'Groats. It took him two days to get there by train, having to spend a night in Glasgow *en route*.

No 3 Squadron had been sent to Wick to defend Scapa Flow and apart from carrying out a lot of convoy patrols, the Squadron was engaged in night flying activities. Ibby found that most of the faces were new because the Squadron had been decimated in France. He managed a couple of flights in a Magister but the CO told him that he couldn't be trained there and he was posted to a Hurricane OTU at Aston Down in the winter of 1940/41. After completing his Hurricane course he was sent to 504 Squadron based at Exeter where he was to meet up again with Wag Haw. It had taken Ibby a full year and a half to be accepted as a fully fledged pilot on a fighter squadron!

* * *

Wag Haw had had better luck than Ibby Waud and found himself on a fighter squadron without any problems along the way. Ibby's troubles had been caused because he had been pushed out of the system through no fault of his own. He was unfortunate to have been sent to a Bomber Command OTU in the first place but having been returned to Flying Training School to gain more night flying experience had made him lose time. Training Command only catered for intakes or courses and not individuals and so Ibby had to join a new intake and do the course all over again.

Wag Haw went through the normal digestive system. When he left his FTS at Sealand he was sent on leave and told to report to a Hurricane Operational Training Unit at Sutton Bridge but received a phone call at home ordering him to join 504 Squadron based at Wick. This dramatic and hurried posting was the first sign that the RAF needed fighter pilots in a hurry and was prepared to short-cut its full training programme. So Haw and his associates including Pilot Officer McGregor and Sergeants Houghton, Holmes, Helk, and Gurteene did their operational training with the Squadron.

504 had been pulled out of the line in France on 20 May when the Squadron had only four serviceable Hurricanes left. Losses had been heavy and the Squadron was in the process of building-up its operational strength when Haw and his associates arrived on the scene. They were fortunate to join a squadron which had just taken part in the new concept of aerial warfare. There is no substitute for battle experience and the replacement pilots were taught the strategy and tactics employed during the 'Blitzkrieg' onslaught.

Many lessons had been learned during those ten days of hectic, non-stop savage fighting over France and Belgium. The vital necessity of having 'weavers' or 'arse-end Charlies' to look out for bouncing Messerschmitts was one. Also, the value of harmonizing Browning .303s at 250 yards instead of the customary 400 yards was another. But there was no question in the minds of Hurricane pilots who had done battle with the Bf 109E that this German fighter had a fantastic performance. It had proved superior to the Hurricane in all respects except for tight turns and manoeuvrability at low altitude. Outclimbed and outdived, their only chance of survival had been to utilize the tight turning circle of their machine to the maximum.

The few weeks before the start of the Battle of Britain gave the replacement pilots a chance of settling down on the Squadron and carrying out their training during a quiet period. But there was some action and Wag Haw in particular had a lucky escape. The Squadron had been moved to Castletown in the most northern part of Scotland where it carried out convoy patrols and was scrambled from time to time to defend Scapa Flow from marauding Heinkel 111s and Ju 88s. It was there that Wag Haw had his first encounter with a German aircraft. One morning at 7.00 am the field telephone rang and pilots were told that radar had spotted an unidentified aircraft. 'A' Flight which was on readiness took off to intercept. The Flight was led by the Flight commander Tony

Rook and included Pilot Officer Frisby and Wag, who was flying arse-end Charlie. The Hurricanes did their usual wobble in formation while pilots pumped up undercarriages and then climbed through layer after layer of cloud.

Suddenly they saw a Heinkel 111 silhouetted against a carpet of grey mist and went down on it. The German pilot dived for cloud cover as the first two Hurricanes attacked and broke away. Wag Haw was the last man in and noticed tracer coming up at him like red hot chain links in the greyness of the day from the gunner of the Heinkel. But he could see that he was well out of range with his first burst so he got in closer and fired again before breaking away. By that time the Heinkel had been swallowed up in the mist and nobody could tell what damage had been done. After landing back at base, however, his ground crew pointed out two holes in his cockpit where a shell had gone clean through — missing him by inches!

In the excitement he couldn't believe it at first and then laughed it off. His narrow squeak, however, was generally regarded as being a splendid show and the boys thought that he was a good chap because he hadn't got himself killed! Apart from that incident Wag was already making his mark with the Squadron. Pilot Officer Frisby had told Tony Rook that he hadn't been able to shake Haw off in mock dog fights, 'You've got a good fighter pilot there', he said.

Perhaps it was because Wag hadn't had the advantages in life which the Auxiliary officers had obviously had which forced him to make himself a better pilot than they. It cost a lot of money to join the Auxiliary clan, especially to maintain social status and Wag had always been conscious of this. They wore an 'A' on their lapels and some of their jackets were lined with red silk which was all part of the image and attitude of an Auxiliary officer. But whenever a party got going Wag was in his element on the piano and this made him the focal point of the 'piss-up'. It was a question of 'Wag, come and play the bloody piano. There's a good chap'. So once he started the rhythm going the atmosphere exploded.

The Squadron atmosphere was essentially competitive, but none of the others could play the piano and this gave Wag an advantage which singled him out amongst the other Sergeant Pilots. But he could also compete with the best of them in the air, as they were beginning to realize. Therefore he was accepted more readily than most by this select fraternity.

The Battle of Britain started officially on 10 July 1940 when 504 Squadron based at Castletown formed part of No 13 Group. The Squadron was held in reserve while the great air battles took place throughout July and August. It was a frustrating and nail-biting business for pilots waiting up there in the far north of Scotland knowing that the chums were being shot down and killed. Everybody desperately wanted to get in on the act but it wasn't until 6 September that the Squadron flew into Hendon, to be put on immediate combat readiness the following day. On that particular day, 23 fighters were lost over Southern England and the Hawker Aircraft factory at Brooklands was bombed though only slight damage was sustained.

504 was the only squadron flying off Hendon and joined 11 Group, coming under the control of North Weald. So the survivors of the Battle for France including Johny Sample, who led the Squadron, Tony Rook, Michael Rook, Jo Royce, Scruffy Royce, Wendell Wilkie, Trevor Parsons, Frisby and others once again squared up to the might of the Luftwaffe. The Squadron was back in business after its traumatic ten days fighting over France some four months previously, but this time its job was to defend London and the South-east of England.

The Squadron had arrived in the line at a time when the resources of Fighter Command were strained to the utmost limit. After almost eight weeks of continuous combat pilots had become physically and mentally exhausted. Very heavy losses had been sustained on both sides and Air Chief Marshal Sir Hugh Dowding had been forced to rearrange his fighter squadrons on the aerial chess board and bring in his last reserves of fresh squadrons fully equipped and ready to fight.

It was in this climate that Wag Haw and his associates, eager and ready for battle, were thrown into the attack on Saturday 7 September. The prime job for Hurricane squadrons was to get at the German bombers, leaving the high performance Spitfires to tackle the Me 109s in the upper regions of the air. There was no shortage of bombers on that day because the Luftwaffe concentrated its attack on London itself and continued to do so until the battle was over.

During the following three weeks, Wag Haw was to open his personal account with the Luftwaffe and achieve his lifelong ambition of becoming a successful wartime fighter pilot. Starting as arse-end Charlie in Squadron formation he was soon leading a section with Sergeant Chan Heywood flying as his number two.

But it was not at all like the scenes he had visualized as a youth when he saw himself shooting down German aircraft on the Western Front.

Wag's introduction to the Battle of Britain began on that fateful Saturday when the Luftwaffe switched tactics and directed its bomber force on London instead of concentrating on wiping out Fighter Command's airfields. The Squadron had had to hang about hours before being brought to 'readiness'. It was a difficult time for everybody and especially those, like Wag, who were going on their first big show.

Wag was keyed up, anxious and ready to go, only waiting to get 'stuck in'. He couldn't help wondering what it was going to be like when he got up there but he wasn't at all frightened or worried about himself. It was a challenge and he had complete confidence in himself after all those months of training. He wondered if those upside down circuits at Brough were going to come in handy when he started to 'mix it' up there.

Outside the Flight hut, the hunchback Hurricanes stood silently in groups, motionless horses waiting for their jockeys against a background of green turf. Pilots sat around the dispersal area in the warm late summer air waiting for the field telephone to ring to announce that the Luftwaffe was on its way. Each man had his own private thoughts as time ticked away and sometimes they wondered whether the bastards would come that day or not. It was nearly 4.00 pm before the Squadron was brought to readiness and shortly afterwards they were ordered to 'scramble'. Radar had picked up a huge formation of nearly 1,000 enemy bombers and fighters approaching London from the east of Sheppey and 21 fighter squadrons based around the city leapt into the air.

Taking off on a 'scramble' is rather like being late for a big party when one makes final adjustments to dress and visage *en route*. There is no time to ponder or think about anything and one gets ready for the occasion almost automatically. As Wag Haw ran towards his Hurricane and clambered into the cockpit: he had only one thing in his mind — and that was not to be left behind.

There were only seconds in which to pull on his helmet, gloves, adjust parachute and harness straps, plug in oxygen and radio leads and clip on oxygen mask before setting the mixture to rich and pitch into fine and opening the throttle, all the while keeping one eye on his chums alongside. Any anxiety had evaporated in the frenzy of activity to get airborne. The Hurricane shivered and trembled as he opened up the throttle against the brakes, throwing up blades of grass and dust which rushed past the open canopy of his cockpit.

It always gave him a great feeling when he took off with the Squadron which he found difficult to put into words. An emotion which he could only describe as a togetherness in that they were all in it and there was no going back or escape. But there was more to it than that when they clawed their way into the air alongside one another. Red, yellow, blue and green sections jockeying into position and eleven other Hurricanes surrounding him each sporting eight Browning machine-guns made him conscious of the fire power and destructive capability of his own fraternity. It gave him a feeling of strength and security although he knew that within seconds they would peel off like leaves in the wind with each man fighting a lone battle.

In the climb his mind and body reacted instinctively to control the machine in Squadron formation. His hands and feet moved in harmony as they did when he played the piano and the vibrations of the Hurricane at full throttle with its spinner pointing to the heavens were transmitted through his body. At 15,000 ft the Squadron levelled out and broke up into two formations in line astern with yellow section providing 'weavers', above and below, whose job it was to look out for Me 109s diving down on them.

He had no time to pause or think about his situation before they spotted waves of bombers ahead and down below flying towards London. Seconds later he heard his CO call 'Tally Ho' and one after the other the Squadron Hurricanes did a wing over and dived down towards the oncoming bombers. When Wag turned his world upside down and went down on the bomber formation he could feel excitement and tension building up inside him. His war had suddenly erupted and through his windscreen he could see that the sky was full of aeroplanes. Layers of twin-engined German raiders sailing along like a giant armada towards the River Thames. As he hurtled down everything happened so quickly that it was as if he was watching a motion picture running at high speed, out of control, and all he could do was to fasten on one particular Dornier bomber and go for it. He made a quarter attack and had it glued in his sights as he closed in and fired. He had to force himself to break away when the Dornier seemed to be rushing at his windscreen like an express train. It was all over in seconds and in breaking away from the German bomber he was immediately aware of his vulnerability to the escorting Me fighters high above. He felt naked and exposed.

Right *Sergeant Ibby Waud at Brough Flying Training School.*

Below *Flying Officer Royce of 504 Squadron with his bulldog during the Battle of Britain.*

Above *Ibby Waud's Heinkel — shot down from Exeter in 1941.*

Below *The CO of 504 Squadron, Johnny Sample, with his famous telescope, passes the time between scrambles outside the Flight hut with Tony Rook.*

Right *Well-crated Hurricane aircraft are hoisted aboard a ship for transport to Russia.*

Below right *Shells and ammunition are also loaded aboard a vessel destined for Russia.*

Above *HMS* Argus — *a converted Italian liner — from which 81 and 134 Squadrons flew off for Russia.*

Left *Ginger 'Eric' Carter flew with his friend John Mulroy into Vianga from Archangel.*

Twisting and turning to catch any sign of a vapour trail or the glint of a sun's ray bouncing off a German fighter's fuselage he snaked his way towards home, twisting his head like a corkscrew. Seconds later and much to his astonishment he saw that the sky had been wiped clean of aircraft, vapour trails and tracer smoke and he was alone.

His face was clammy inside his oxygen mask and he was sweating from the exertion of throwing his machine around the sky. His radio was crackling away and he was flying his Hurricane automatically as if it was strapped to his arse, allowing him full freedom to comb the open sky for any sign of movement. Those ninety seconds or more of rigid concentration when he had closed in on that Dornier had left him feeling elated beyond measure.

After landing he was de-briefed by the Intelligence officer but all he could say was that he thought he had pumped a lot of lead into a Dornier. By that time it was clear that London was the target and the Luftwaffe was putting in maximum effort. It wasn't long before Wag Haw was scrambled again and the Squadron vectored towards Tilbury and Thames Haven where fires were breaking out in the dockland area.

Saturday 7 September, turned out to be a memorable day for 504. The Squadron had been catapulted into the Battle of Britain on the very day that the Luftwaffe had switched tactics and sent over massive daylight formations to bomb British cities. Thirty-one British fighters went down during the initial onslaught upon London and the Germans lost 39 aircraft during the day. Wag Haw and his chums who joined 504 as replacement pilots following the Battle for France found themselves in a frenzy of action which continued without respite until dusk. Pilot Officer McGregor, for example, who had trained with Wag at Sealand spent over four hours in his Hurricane that day having been scrambled four times. But, for all their efforts, by the time the last Hurricane had flopped down onto the grass airfield at Hendon the city and dockland skyline was silhouetted against a wall of pulsating flames.

After high tea in the Sergeants' Mess, Wag and his chum Chan Heywood made for the nearest pub and found themselves in the Hendon Hall Hotel. For them it was a necessity to get right away from the airfield atmosphere and have a 'piss-up'. Their reception was embarrassing because the locals knew that a fighter squadron had flown into Hendon the day before and they must be part of it. They weren't allowed to buy a drink and Wag was soon on the piano with everybody singing in party mood.

He was playing 'Roll out the Barrel' when the air raid sirens wailed out heralding a cycle of night bombing which was to continue until half past four in the morning. Bombs whistled down, glasses rattled and shivered on the shelves and occasionally the building shuddered but nobody seemed inclined to leave the pub and make for the shelters. The crowd kept sending beer over to the pilots only pausing now and then when they heard an extra loud crump from a bomb nearby.

It was an atmosphere which was to characterize their lives during the next three weeks. A hectic frothy mixture of aerial combat by day and blitz parties at night. There was no opportunity to get away from it all and recuperate. The adrenalin had to flow all the time gradually winding them up into a state of physical and nervous exhaustion. This had already happened to many of the pilots in those Regular and Auxiliary squadrons which had been continually in action since the battle began in early July.

Like other squadrons, 504 lost pilots and others had narrow escapes. Frisby, Wendel Wilkie, Gurteene and Helke had gone down. Basil Bush had a shell go straight through his windscreen which shattered it but somehow he managed to bring his aircraft back and had to have glass removed from his eye. Artie Holmes's scrap over the West End of London was quite a remarkable affair. He had engaged two Dorniers and had run out of ammunition when he saw a Heinkel — which he rammed. The German bomber crashed in the environs of Victoria Station and Artie baled out and landed in a dustbin. King George VI had watched the action from Buckingham Palace and asked to meet the pilot concerned, which Holmes found even more frightening!

During those three weeks of combat from Hendon, Wag Haw's natural aptitude as an aggressive fighter pilot who could really handle his machine manifested itself. He was soon leading a section with Chan Heywood flying as his number two and he was given his own squadron aircraft, 'H' for Harry — a sign of approval making him a fully fledged member of the team.

He was also beginning to know some of the officers a little better especially those who occasionally joined him around the piano in the party sessions at the local pub. 'Scruffy' Royce often drifted in with his spotted bulldog which everybody admired although some found it rather odd that anyone should have a bulldog on a fighter station. It was, however, symbolic of the Auxiliary attitude, rather like the CO's large telescope which he kept at Flights. Johnny

Sample would probably have been better off with a pair of binoculars but that wasn't the point. The brass telescope and the bulldog were all part of the image, as were their tunics lined with red silk and displaying gold 'A' badges on their lapels.

The Battle of Britain reached its crescendo on 15 September with the Luftwaffe still sending huge formations of bombers and fighters to crack London. This had enabled Fighter Command to pull in every available squadron from outlying areas where they had been defending airfields and concentrate totally on breaking up the mass attacks. Consequently, the big German formations faced Fighter Command at maximum strength with time to refuel and re-arm its fighters between morning and afternoon attacks. The day's tally was indicative: 27 British fighters were lost against 56 German aircraft destroyed.

On 26 September, 504 Squadron was ordered to fly to Filton — home of the Bristol Aeroplane Company on the outskirts of Bristol — which had been heavily bombed on the previous day. The Germans had been particularly clever in catching Filton when it had no fighter protection. It was common knowledge in the locality that fighter squadrons were being changed over. On the following day 504 Squadron was scrambled to intercept a bomber force of Me 110s heading towards Bristol. There were over forty of them but 504 broke up the formation, shooting down five 110s and thwarting the raid.

Wag himself shot one down and in the general melee noticed his cylinder head temperature going up rather rapidly, from which he assumed that somebody had clobbered him. There was only one thing that he could do and that was to switch off and disappear without attracting the attention of a Me 110. He broke away by stalling his Hurricane and spinning down, leaving it rather late before he straightened out. Fortunately there was no sign of any bandit closing in to finish him off and he chose a large cornfield for a belly landing.

The Hurricane smelt hot and without the usual throaty roar from the Rolls-Royce Merlin engine the silence was uncanny. All he could hear was the rushing of the wind as he locked back his cockpit hood and made sure that his harness straps were secured. Systematically, he unplugged his RT and oxygen leads to free himself. It was the first time that he had ever belly landed an aircraft and he was worried about catching fire as he made his approach. Out of the corner of an eye he noticed a horse pulling a reaping maching as he floated into the field and tore into the high standing corn. He kept the stick forward and dug the nose into the earth to stop her ballooning and he could feel the pressure on his body as she slewed this way and that before grinding to a standstill. He didn't waste a second before leaping out and running away from his aircraft, scared that she might blow up at any minute.

He flung himself down in the corn, panting with the exertion of making ground in his parachute harness. Taking off his helmet and gloves he lay there sweating and he was unable to stop his right knee trembling and pulsating. This twitching of his knee worried him and it had occurred several times previously after aerial combat. He had never suffered from it in the air and it came on after he had landed. At first he hadn't taken any notice thinking that he must have strained a nerve or tendon in his leg by pushing too hard on the rudder pedal but it persisted and he daren't mention it to anybody.

He could feel his knee jumping when the farmer who had been reaping the corn suddenly appeared and stood there glaring at him without saying a word. Wag told him that he wasn't a German but an English fighter pilot. In response the man took off his rather battered hat and scratched the back of his head with a sullen expression on his face. The chap was obviously a farm labourer and Wag could see that he wasn't exactly delighted that his beautiful crop of corn had been carved up by a Hurricane.

Still the man remained speechless glancing around at the devastation in his field. It was a farcical situation and as Wag got to his feet he asked where the nearest road was so that he could cadge a lift. The scarecrow of a man pointed in the direction and still without a word walked off towards his horse.

Slinging his parachute over his shoulder and carrying his helmet, Wag started walking through the cornfield. His knee had stopped trembling and he couldn't help laughing to himself at the reception he had received after shooting down a German bomber and then having to crash land. Even thinking about it made him giggle as if he was slightly pissed. Anyway, he had been bloody lucky because the high standing corn had slowed his Hurricane down when he belly landed. Then he remembered that he hadn't got a penny in his pocket and he had no idea where he was.

His luck was in because a Ford 8 drew up and the driver, somewhat astonished to see a young man standing on the roadside in flying gear, offered to give him a lift into Taunton. From there he told Wag that he could catch a train to Bristol. Wag thought himself fortunate to get a lift because petrol rationing meant there were few cars on the road. The driver explained that he was an agricultural seeds salesman so he got extra coupons. They drove for well over half-an-hour without seeing anything on the road, not even signposts which had been painted out to confuse German parachutists. When they eventually arrived in Taunton the man insisted on buying Wag lunch and they stopped at the County Hotel.

It was getting rather late but the first thing on Wag's mind was to get stuck in to some beer and iron out the creases in his system. He soon attracted a crowd of people, mostly farmers, who wanted to buy him a drink and ask questions. He felt shy, tense, emotionally drained and self-conscious when they gathered round him. His mental processes seemed to have seized up and he found himself repeating clipped RAF jargon saying quite simply that he had clobbered an Me 110 and had to pancake in a cornfield but the whole thing had been 'a piece of cake' really.

As the beer and food did its work he began to feel better and enjoyed the party which went on into the late afternoon. He telephoned Filton and told the boys that he was quietly getting pissed and they laid on a truck to pick him up at Temple Meads station. The crowd was surprised and disappointed when he refused a bed for the night but it had all been a good show and he left in high spirits.

On the way back to Bristol he began to feel a little jaded and introspective. Fragments of his dogfight with the Me 110s stabbed into his mind until they virtually completed a jigsaw of the action. He could see those twin-engined Messerschmitts flashing across his windscreen until he got one in his sights and hung onto it like a limpet, feeling the pressure on his body from gravity as his speed built up and he tightened the turn. Concentrating rigidly on drawing his bead through that German aircraft until he could fire ahead of its nose, he pressed the gun button feeling the wings of his Hurricane vibrating. A split second when he knew for certain that his bullets were raking the German and then with stick and rudder he skidded away, fighting for his own survival.

He had been bloody scared at the time but in thinking back he recognized and admitted to himself that he had always experienced spasms of terror in frenzied moments of combat. It seemed odd to him that after the evening piss-ups he genuinely looked forward to doing it all over again on the following day as if he was some kind of masochist trying to beat hell out of himself.

Sitting back in the train he concluded that aerial combat, as far as he was concerned, acted like a drug which he had to keep on taking for his own satisfaction. He was scared during the action itself and he supposed that most of the others were but nobody mentioned it. Being frightened, he thought, was something one could overcome but having the cold finger of fear penetrate one's body like a cancer was something quite different.

When the train pulled into Temple Meads Station the blackout was on and he very nearly got out of the carriage door on the wrong side of the train. He had been struggling to extricate himself with his parachute slung over his shoulder when somebody yelled, 'I wouldn't get out that side, mate. If I was you.'

*　　*　　*

The use of Me 110s in a bomber role escorted by high-flying Me 109s in late September marked a new phase in Luftwaffe aerial strikes by day. The fast 109 fighters no longer had to slow down as they had previously done when escorting Heinkels and Dorniers and lightning strikes on selected targets such as aircraft factories formed part of the new tactics. These factories, including Supermarine, Hawker and Bristol, were all attacked during the week of 21 September. Over 250 people were killed, many of them when an air raid shelter received a direct hit during the raid on the Bristol Aeroplane Company at Filton on the 26th. The Bristol company was particularly grateful to 504 Squadron who broke up another attack on the following day before Me 110 fighter bombers reached their Filton target. The Squadron was presented with a commemorative ashtray machined out of a highly polished cylinder head and was given lunch.

With the advent of high-altitude, high-speed fighter bomber strikes the large formation daylight attacks faded out. The Me 110 replaced the Heinkel and Dornier by day leaving the main bomber force to carry out a regular cycle of night attacks concentrating on London. The Battle of Britain was approaching its final stages and Fighter Command was already thinking about plans for an offensive strategy to carry the war into enemy-occupied territory on the other side of the English Channel.

Wag Haw and his RAFVR associates who joined 504 Squadron had entered the battle fresh and eager for a scrap at a crucial stage when the climax was coming and the outcome was in the balance. During the months of August and September when the thin blue line became stretched to the utmost limit and sometimes beyond, replacements from the RAFVR played a life-saving role in keeping the line intact.

Fighter Command preserved the Auxiliary squadrons as units which was an important factor in maintaining an *esprit de corps* beyond price. 504 Squadron was a typical example. Led by Johnny Sample who was a regular officer, the Squadron included two sets of brothers, the Rooks and Royces, and others who came from the same area with similar backgrounds. They were a moneyed, elite group able to enjoy a full social life in a lighthearted prankish way. Understatement and non-conformity were the name of the game and satirizing pomposity and discipline was all part of the attitude. Most fighter pilots had many of these characteristics but Auxiliary squadrons cultivated them to a marked degree and being an 'Auxiliary' meant that one was a member of a gentlemen's club where the family atmosphere and status were paramount.

Sergeant Wag Haw having already distinguished himself as a fighter pilot was beginning to wonder what he would have to do in order to get himself a commission. He realized that he would have to become an officer if he was going to get anywhere in the RAF and he was determined to make the Service his career if he survived the war. He put in a request to the Squadron Adjutant to ask for an official meeting with his commanding officer, Squadron Leader Sample, in order to seek his advice.

Despite the fact that Squadron pilots including the CO and his Flight commanders lounged about in an informal atmosphere at Flights waiting for the field telephone to ring it was not the done thing for a Sergeant to approach his CO. Formality and etiquette were the keynotes in the game and there was a wide gulf between officers and other ranks.

Wag Haw had thought the matter over carefully, accepting the fact that he might have to modify his broad Yorkshire accent and adopt a more sophisticated attitude. His main contention was that he was as good if not better than any of them in the air and there was no reason why he shouldn't become one of them. During his interview the CO told him not unkindly that there was no question of his getting a commission at that juncture and suggested that he should concentrate on winning a Distinguished Flying Medal and then re-apply. Wag went away without any recriminations determined to shoot more Germans down and get himself a DFM in the process. In looking back he thought that Johnny Sample had probably done him a favour because he would have felt like a fish out of water in the Officers' Mess at that stage in his combat career but at least he had had the satisfaction and guts to have a go.

As the Battle of Britain finally came to an end the weather began to deteriorate. 504 Squadron remained at Filton carrying out interceptions to combat lightning bombing strikes and were scrambled on many occasions, often in bad weather. The airfield was surrounded by barrage balloons which made life extremely difficult especially when visibility was poor. When the Squadron was scrambed, for example, a barrage balloon had to be pulled down and then put up again when the Hurricanes had vanished and the operation repeated to allow them to land.

During that period pilots spent a lot of flying time being vectored around the area in cloud, only occasionally getting a sniff of action. There were a few skirmishes but no kills. Pilot Officer McGregor, who had trained with Wag at Sealand, chased a Ju 88 and attacked it over Guernsey but became lost in cloud and finally landed at Manston having been airborne for over two hours. This was the kind of action which the Squadron experienced and found rather frustrating after the frenzied aerial battles from Hendon.

Wag in his enthusiasm and determination to get in as many flying hours as possible volunteered for anything going and often got his chance when the weather was duff. So much so that when the clouds were on the deck and the field telephone rang the boys used to say, 'Send off Cloudy Jo' — meaning Wag, of course.

Flying in cloud for any length of time was bloody hard work as Wag discovered when he had a lengthy session flying number two to Scruffy Royce on one November morning. The barrage balloons were lost in cloud and viz was down to a few hundred yards when they were scrambled. The two Hurricanes disappeared into mist shortly after leaving the deck and Wag tucked himself behind and below Scruffy concentrating on his leader's navigation lights while automatically adjusting his controls in the climb.

He had no problem at first because he was enveloped in light mist and the air was smooth allowing him to fly his machine with only light pressure on the stick and rudder pedals. He could see by his altimeter that they were climbing but that was all. Gradually it got darker and more bumpy so that he had to take a firmer grip on the controls and concentrate harder on Scruffy's two nav lights above him.

As the air got more turbulent he found himself working hard to maintain station behind Scruffy but he had no idea where they were or their position in flight. There was no horizon, earth or sky, only a blanket of darkness. His guiding lights were two dim little stars on the edges of Scruffy's wingtips which became blurred at times from driving rain on his windscreen. Looking up he could make out the vague shape of his leader's underbelly and tailplane bouncing up and down like a yo-yo. All he could do was to keep his eyes riveted on those lights and fly by the seat of his pants. He couldn't relax for a second and at one stage the surrounding cloud was so black and the turbulence so violent that he had to fight hard to control the machine. Scruffy's Hurricane appeared to be having convulsions by the way it was cavorting about and he found himself pumping his throttle and working his stick and rudder incessantly to keep his distance and avoid collision. But he was determined not to break away and have to call up control for a homing. That would have been an admission of defeat.

The flight seemed interminable when he sensed that they were descending and the cloud got a little lighter. The continual bumping about slackened off and it became easier to keep station. It was only then that he realized how rigid he had been on the controls and how tensed up he was. His arms and legs ached and he had no idea how long the two aircraft had been up there.

It was a relief when they broke cloud at about 400 ft and came in to land into a strong and gusty wind. As they walked into Flights Scruffy Royce patted him on the back and told him that he had put up a good show. It was a nice gesture on Scruffy's part made even more acceptable because it was carried out in front of the others. Shortly afterwards the CO, Johnny Sample, announced that the weather had closed in and the Squadron had been 'stood down' for the rest of the day.

*   *   *

While no official date was given to mark the ending of the Battle of Britain it is generally considered that by early November the immediate threat of a German invasion was unlikely. Most people felt that they were living on borrowed time and that the Germans had only postponed the inevitable. There was no doubt in the minds of the general public that the Luftwaffe had failed to destroy Fighter Command and the battle had been a great victory for the young British fighter pilots. For the first time in the history of warfare a projected invasion on a large scale had been neutralized by air power alone and the fighter had been the dominating piece on the military chessboard.

Its aftermath left a dangerously depleted Fighter Command and a disillusioned and battered Luftwaffe which had previously suffered substantial losses during the collapse of France. Victory gave the RAF an unprecedented boost and uplift. Thousands of young men at home and throughout the free world had been captivated by the exploits of 'the few' and set their sights on becoming fighter pilots. The aerial battles over Southern England had sown the seeds which, carried by the media to Canada, Australia, New Zealand, South Africa and to other countries including America, came to fruition in the Empire Air Training Scheme.

During the winter of 1940 and up to the early summer of '41, 504 Squadron had primarily played a defensive role in carrying out interceptions and convoy patrols. This was because their elderly Mark I Hurricanes were considered unsuitable for offensive operations across Northern France. Apart from this the Squadron had been engaged in a little bomber escort work and night patrols. Pilots had been anxiously waiting to be converted onto the Hurricane Mark IIC which had an increased performance and was equipped with four 20mm cannons.

It wasn't until late July that the Squadron was posted to Fairwood Common, outside Swansea, to do the conversion course. It was then that the whole of 'A' Flight was transferred to 81 Squadron and a new 504 Squadron was built up from 'B' Flight. Wag Haw and his associates from 'A' Flight who had been posted to 81 Squadron were told that they were going overseas. Nobody had any idea then that they would shortly be on their way to the Arctic Circle and find themselves in the desolate tundra region of North Russia flying off an airfield in the proximity of Murmansk.

Chapter 2
Murmansk

Operation 'Sea Lion', the code name for the German invasion of England, had been shelved in mid-September 1940 when the Germans began dismantling air transport facilities in Holland. The attention of the German High Command then became focused for the next eight and a half months on planning the invasion of Russia known as 'Operation Barbarossa'. In his Directive No 21, dated 18 December 1940, Hitler said that the German Wehrmacht must be prepared, even before conclusion of the war against Britain, to overthrow Soviet Russia by a rapid campaign.

One would have expected that prime targets including Moscow, Leningrad, Kiev and Rostov would be on the list of strategic objectives but it was difficult to understand at first glance why the town of Murmansk should have been bracketed alongside those great cities which constituted the very heart of Russia. Little-known Murmansk appeared to be a small port on the coastline of Northern Russia surrounded by tundra country and frozen wastelands. Hardly a target of great significance in the projected German invasion of Russia!

During the planning stages of 'Operation Barbarossa', however, Adolf Hitler took a personal interest in Murmansk and regarded it as the most dangerous Russian deployment centre in the far northern territory. He had good reasons for so doing in that the port was free of ice throughout the year and provided a gateway into the Atlantic, the railway system supplied a communications network from the Arctic Ocean into Central Russia and the town itself was the only heavily defended strongpoint in a thinly populated area. Apart from that, the valuable nickel mines at Petsamo were only sixty miles west of Murmansk and Kirknes on the Varangeren Fiord in Norway another thirty miles beyond. The northern extremities of Norway, Finland and Russia converged in the general area around Varangeren Fiord. Hitler realized that if the Russians, who occupied Finland, were to break through the short distance to the fiord then they could threaten the Arctic Ocean and his ports in occupied Northern Norway. He was well aware that Stalin could use the Murmansk railway to move men and supplies quickly from Central Russia to the Finnish border to back up any such attack and that the nickel mines of Petsamo would be a rich prize. Therefore, he decided that Murmansk had to be captured at the very outset of the Eastern campaign and could see no reason why his Mountain Jägers should have any major difficulties in advancing sixty miles from the Finnish border to Murmansk itself.

It is quite extraordinary that Hitler should overlook a historical event which happened in 1917 when America became Russia's ally in the war against the Kaiser's Germany. It was then that Murmansk with its ice-free port and railway communication links provided the shortest route and vital supply line between America and Russia. He did not foresee that history was going to repeat itself in a most remarkable and devastating way as far as he was concerned in that Murmansk and the port of Archangel on the White Sea were to take in vast quantities of British and American aid and play a major part in Russia's survival. So much so that one convoy arriving in the port of Murmansk could make up Russian losses of military equipment and supplies from a major battle.

Although Archangel is further south than Murmansk it is blocked by ice for three months of the year leaving Murmansk as the only ice-free port with access to the Atlantic. This strange phenomenon of nature which leaves Murmansk open is entirely due to the warm waters of the Gulf Stream. These waters pass through the gap between Greenland and Norway and swirl round the top of the Norwegian coast and into the Kola Bay where lies the port of Murmansk. This ensures that the Kola Bay never freezes up even in the depths of the Arctic winter when temperatures can get down to 50 degrees or more below zero.

Two months before 'Operation Barbarossa' began, Hitler talked with General Dietl who commanded 'Mountain Corps Norway'. He wanted to know how things were progressing as far as the plans for the northern operation were concerned. Dietl made no bones about the problems which confronted him and did his best to make his Führer aware of the landscape in the tundra area surrounding Murmansk and the arctic conditions that prevailed.

Hitler, like most Germans, knew little or nothing about arctic conditions but listened patiently while Dietl made his points. The sixty miles of tundra belt surrounding Murmansk he described as a pathless, stony desert with nothing but rocks and scree: a wilderness bordering on a myriad of lakes, rivers and rapids; a swamp infested by mosquitoes during three short summer months under hot sun and in winter nothing but blast frozen landscape swept by icy gales. According to Dietl those sixty miles from the Finnish border to Murmansk were nothing but a hell on earth in which conditions for waging war were impossible.

In a forthright and simple manner he tried to dissuade Hitler from attacking the town of Murmansk and encouraged his Führer to allow him to concentrate his divisions on defending the Petsamo area which was economically and strategically vital. The railway lines leading to Murmansk, he argued, could be cut further south in more favourable country and this in itself would isolate the town. He pointed out that the Russians had supply bases directly behind their front across the Petsamo line and that back-up and supplies in this type of country would be key factors.

'We have to bring in everything', he said, 'by sea from Hamburg and the Baltic ports to the Gulf of Bothnia and on up the Arctic Ocean Road through Finland by tortuous routes to Petsamo.' 'But even then,' he stated quietly, 'our supplies would have to be brought up to the front line by lorry, horse-drawn cart, mules and finally manhandled to positions. Cutting the railway line', he explained, 'would leave the Russians in a similar position to ourselves!'

Hitler was impressed but in spite of what Dietl had to say he ordered that the main drive of the North Russian campaign was first to occupy the Petsamo area and then to advance across the tundra and take Murmansk. 'Operation Platinum Fox' was the code name given for the assault on Murmansk and this was to start a week after Dietl's Mountain Jägers had occupied the nickel mines area of Petsamo.

The General did at least succeed in making his point about cutting the Murmansk rail links because Hitler directed that six divisions be employed to cut the railway line at three different points further south. In addition, Dietl received the support of twelve detachments of the Reich Labour Service to provide extra muscle power and to back up his forces. But Hitler had disregarded Dietl's basic argument not to attack Murmansk and simply cut the town's supply lines.

While Dietl was making his final preparations for his Arctic campaign, German troops were massing on the Russian border along a front of over 900 miles from the Baltic to the Black Sea. Everything had to be carried out with complete operational secrecy as the two countries had signed a non-aggression pact in 1939 just before Germany had invaded Poland and both had been watching one another like hawks during this fragile alliance.

Hitler was well aware that Stalin was in the middle of a frantic rearmament and mobilization programme and that the time was ripe for an attack but his major problem was to ensure that German forces should take full advantage of the Russian summer. He had to gamble everything on a lightning victory before the Russian winter descended.

Soviet Intelligence had been reporting a rapid build-up of German forces along the border but Stalin refused to make any move of provocation and was, like Chamberlain in 1939, playing for time. He was forced into that situation because most of his arms and equipment were obsolete. His army had only about 1,500 of the new KV and T-34 tanks and his air force had a like number of modern machines. The MiG-3, the fastest of his fighters, was currently being introduced to squadrons as part of the re-equipment programme. He had no radar systems and radio communications were very primitive. To back up his modern equipment he had thousands of lighter tanks and a large number of second line aircraft.

Hitler had few problems. His 'Blitzkrieg' techniques had proved successful since the days of the Spanish Civil War. Nothing had been able to prevent the German military machine from rolling across Europe during 1939 and '40. By mid '41 his forces were reporting victories in Greece, North Africa and Yugoslavia. It seemed at that time that the German soldier was invincible and nothing would stop Hitler in his conquest of Europe.

Goering was one of the few men who wanted Hitler to defer his attack on Russia until the Luftwaffe had had a chance to recuperate and build up its strength following losses sustained during the fall of France and the Battle of Britain. Such losses were probably in the region of about 2,500 aircraft but even more important was the fact that the Germans had lost a battle and the Luftwaffe was 'carrying the can' for it. Nevertheless, the Luftwaffe was able to amass some 2,000 or more aircraft to start the campaign.

In order to achieve complete secrecy German Intelligence had gone to great lengths to convince troops camping alongside the Russian and Ukranian border that they were being rested prior to the Invasion of Britain. Thousands of maps were distributed revealing the invasion plan. Code names of 'Harpoon' and 'Shark' identified special operations and English interpreters joined units to explain the invasion strategy in great detail. Rumours were circulated about airborne units which would be dropping on selective targets and a pre-invasion atmosphere of excitement and dedication to the Fatherland was skilfully created amongst the troops. The German propaganda machine poured out a steady stream of anti-British abuse and for once in a while there was no comment against the Soviet system.

While the primary excuse for so many German divisions massing along the Russian border was explained away as being a run-up to the invasion of England some German units were told that they were standing by to be allowed to pass through Russian territory on their way to attack India. Others were informed that Stalin had leased the Ukraine to Hitler and they were going in as the army of occupation.

At eleven o'clock on the Saturday morning of 21 June 1941, Adolf Hitler gave the order for 'Operation Barbarossa' to be put into action. By ten o'clock that evening three million German soldiers knew that they were going to attack the Soviet Union first thing on the following morning. A free issue of booze, tobacco and chocolate helped many of them while away the time before zero hour when the guns would start and they would be 'going over the top'.

Earlier that evening an extraordinary event had taken place on the Russian front. A German Sergeant-Major had come over to Russian frontier guards and told them that German troops were moving into position and that the invasion would begin on the following morning. The news was immediately transmitted to High Command and Marshal Zhukov and others went to the Kremlin to see Stalin to show him the draft of a directive they had drawn up to combat the situation.

Stalin was hesitant about alerting all troops along the border pointing out that the Sergeant-Major's action might well be a ruse to provoke a conflict. He thought that it was too premature to issue such a document, saying that perhaps the question could still be handled peacefully. We must give a short directive, he said, stating that an attack may begin with provocative actions by the German forces. The troops of the border districts must not fall for any provocation, and avoid complications. Eventually a compromise was reached putting troops on full combat readiness but without giving them the authority to retaliate.

The document signed by Timoshenko and Zhukov was transmitted at 00.30 hours on Sunday 22 June, three hours before war erupted. About that time the command post at Ternopol came through and announced that a German soldier from the 222nd Infantry Regiment had swum the river and told frontier guards that the Germans were going to attack at 4.00 am. It was becoming increasingly obvious that German divisions were moving up to the frontier.

Long before dawn crept across the eastern sky Luftwaffe aircrews had climbed into their machines and were standing by for take-off. Aircraft had been scheduled to be over their targets and ready to attack the moment that the guns opened up along the front. Saboteurs had been busy before daybreak cutting telephone cables and placing charges to destroy communication links. Nothing was left to chance.

The situation way up north in Murmansk territory under the midnight sun was more complicated. General Dietl's men in Norway had to cross Finnish territory before they could get to the Russian border and Finland was occupied by Russia. There was a Russian consul in Petsamo and he was bound to report back any troop movements. It was essential that as soon as war started Dietl's sappers should be working on the bridging of the Petsamo river. By arrangement with the Finns a company of sappers wearing civilian clothes moved across Finnish territory and waited at the frontier. Once 'Operation Barbarossa' started and Germany was at war with Russia the guards lifted the barrier and the sappers moved off.

Without any declaration of war and on the dot of 3.30 am, thousands of German guns opened up along a front of 1,500 or so miles. The earth vomited great showers of dust and muck as the softening up process began. Behind the shells German infantry and mechanized units began to move into Russia. The Luftwaffe in its role as the advanced striking force was already bombing towns, airfields, troop concentrations and communications networks. The Blitzkrieg machine had started to roll forward and gather momentum. Shortly after 04.30, the German Ambassador

Count von der Schulenburg handed Molotov a note to the effect that the German government had declared war on the Soviet Union.

Initial Luftwaffe attacks caught Russian field commanders in a dilemma because they had been specifically ordered not to respond to provocation. Their men were under a hail of bombs and machine-gun fire without being able to retaliate. Unlike their German counterparts, the vast majority of Russian soldiers had never been in action and they found themselves crouching down in slit trenches while the earth around vibrated and heaved with bomb blasts. The air was filled with flying particles and the sickly smell of cordite seeped into their nostrils. All they could do was to sweat it out and wait for orders.

It wasn't until 08.00 that Soviet forces were told officially over the radio that Germany had attacked Russia and that they were to counter attack. This confusion and delay enabled German armour to drive wedges of up to 50 kilometres into Russian defences and Panzer divisions to gain momentum.

As the minutes and hours ticked away on that Sunday morning the German military machine took full advantage of the chaotic situation in which Russian forces found themselves. Some Russian front line units had no radio links: others could not communicate because lines had been cut by saboteurs; there was no co-ordinated defence strategy; aircraft had been unable to take off and disperse to field strips and precious time had been lost in waiting for orders to open fire and counter attack.

From the outset the Luftwaffe had gained control of the air and blasted a path for the Panzer divisions and mechanized infantry units. In so doing it inflicted severe damage on the Red Air Force and destroyed hundreds of aircraft on the ground. German pilots could scarcely believe their eyes when they saw Russian aircraft lined up like sitting ducks on airfields ripe for a stick of bombs or a low-level straffing run. It was relatively simple for experienced Luftwaffe pilots to create maximum mayhem in situations like these. Control of the air was the prime factor in allowing the Luftwaffe full freedom to carry out pre-emptive strikes on ground targets ahead of the advancing troops.

By lunchtime there was still no precise information about how far or to what extent German armoured divisions had driven wedges into Soviet territory. Russian commanders were desperately trying to organize counter attacks but owing to poor communications and lack of a master strategy these could not be co-ordinated. Orders were given and countermanded time and again and whenever Russian tanks massed for a major counter-thrust they received a devastating aerial onslaught from Heinkels, Dorniers, Ju 88s, Messerschmitts and Stuka dive bombers. At lunch time, Stalin informed Zhukov, Shaposhnikov and Kulik that the Politburo had decided to send them to various sections of the front as representatives of High Command and that they were to take off at once.

News of the German invasion had been radioed across the world shortly after the artillery barrage had begun at 03.30. Winston Churchill had known for some time that a German invasion of Russia was imminent. He had recently been informing Stalin of major air traffic movements from the Balkans to the Russian frontier. Only three days previously he had telegraphed Roosevelt to say that major German forces had massed along a line from Finland in the north right down to Rumania in the south and that air and armoured forces were currently moving into position. He also made it clear to Roosevelt that Britain would give all encouragement and help that she could spare to the Russians.

Churchill was given the news of the invasion at 8.00 am. He was relieved and delighted because the Germans were going to be totally committed in that theatre which would naturally take the pressure off Britain for a while. Personally he thought that in the final outcome the Soviets would be defeated and voiced this opinion to some of his close associates.

Only yesterday, Saturday 21 June, Russia had been, in effect, an enemy of Britain, having signed a non-aggression pact with Hitler in 1939. Overnight she had become an ally but Churchill was conscious that many British people wouldn't want to be too closely associated with Russia on political grounds. But Anglo/American aid for the Russians would prove vital in helping them prolong their fight for survival. His prime object was to smash the Nazi war machine and this transcended all other considerations including his basic hatred of the worst features of Communism.

Any alliance or partnership with Russia, he concluded, would have to be on a military basis from the outset. There was no time for him to air the situation or prepare the ground in cabinet before making his broadcast to the nation and it was his decision alone to go ahead.

That Sunday, 22 June, when he was preparing his radio broadcast must have been one of the most difficult days in Winston Churchill's life, wondering, perhaps, from time to time while carefully choosing his words, how his party, parliament, the press and most important of all how the great British public would react after his microphone had been switched off. He was restless to a degree, sounding opinion amongst colleagues at Chequers and phoning others for their spontaneous reaction having already made up his mind not only to give Russia all the help in Britain's power but to put maximum pressure on America to do the same.

Whenever a Churchill broadcast was in the offing the entire nation gathered round radios and 'cocked an ear', waiting in suspense. As Big Ben chimed nine times and its booming sound faded on that warm summer evening, a blanket of silence clamped down on the length and breadth of the land. There was a few moments hush before he was formally announced when his listeners couldn't help wondering what triumphs or disasters might lie in store for them.

Churchill began by talking about his hatred of Communism since the Bolshevik revolution of 1917 and likened its worst features to the evils of the Nazi regime. No one, he said, had been more anti-Communist than himself over the past 25 years and never would he unsay one word that he had spoken in the past.

This was an extraordinary opening to a speech in which Churchill was to make a declaration that British policy was to give all the aid we could to Russia and the Russian people. It was a clever move, however, on Churchill's part to identify himself as a leading anti-Communist, thus eliciting the support of all those who had no time for the Marxist doctrine — and there were many of them. But having made his personal views about Communism abundantly clear, Churchill used all his oratorical skills to present an emotional picture of the Russian scene and the desperate plight in which the Russian people found themselves:

'I see the Russian soldiers standing on the threshold of their native land, guarding the fields which their fathers have tilled from time immemorial. I see them guarding their homes where mothers and wives pray — ha, yes, for there are times when all pray — for the safety of their loved ones, the return of the bread-winner, of their champion, of their protector. I see the 10,000 villages of Russia where the means of existence is wrung so hardly from the soil, but where there are still primordial human joys, where maidens laugh and children play.

'I see advancing upon all this in hideous onslaught the Nazi war machine, with its clanking, heel-clicking, dandified Prussian officers, its craft expert agents fresh from the cowing and tying down of a dozen countries. I see also the dull, drilled, docile, brutish masses of the Hun soldiery plodding on like a swarm of crawling locusts. I see the German bombers and fighters in the sky, still smarting from many a British whipping, delighted to find what they believe is an easier and safer prey.

Churchill then proceeded to the main plank of his argument which was that: 'Any man or state who fights on against Nazidom will have our aid. Any man or state who marches with Hitler is our foe'. The Russian danger, he concluded, was our danger and the danger of the United States and therefore we must strike with united strength. His speech was generally regarded amongst politicians and public alike as having been 'a masterpiece'.

*   *   *

Churchill was right in his broadcast when he foresaw the Nazi war machine advancing in hideous onslaught. The first day of the invasion ended with Russian frontier armies in disarray and many of them facing a grave situation. The German plan, an essentially simple one was being carried out with ruthless efficiency. Army Group North, under von Leeb was to move towards Leningrad, von Bock's Army Group Centre towards Moscow and Army Group South commanded by von Rundstedt had the grain, coal and mineral area of the Ukraine as its objective.

On the northern flank, General Dietl led the Arctic campaign aided by the Finns under General Mannheim and in the south, the German Army of von Schoberth, together with the Rumanians under Marshal Antonescu, were to liberate the eastern provinces which had been occupied by the Russians.

Hitler gambled that his 'Blitzkrieg' technique would carve through Russian defences and that he would take Moscow within a couple of months. He believed that his initial sledgehammer assault against frontier forces would compel the Russians to move up their main armies in order to hold the line. This, he considered, would enable him to encircle heavy Russian concentrations and decimate them. But in the event the Russians were caught completely by surprise, without proper communications and were unable to move up their main armies to block German break-outs in the frontier areas.

Marshal Zukhov wrote in his memoirs: 'I do not venture to state what would have happened if this were done: whether the result would have been better or worse. It is quite possible that being under-equipped with anti-tank and anti-aircraft facilities and being less mobile than the enemy, our troops may have failed to withstand the powerful slashing thrusts of the enemy Panzer forces and may therefore, have found themselves in as grave a predicament as some of the armies of the frontier districts.'

The Russians had strengthened their defences in the southern sector assuming that Hilter would make his major thrust towards the Ukraine but the Führer had decided otherwise. As, unexpectedly, he had by-passed the Maginot line when storming across the Low Countries, so he chose Moscow as his prime target and launched his heaviest assault in that direction. During the next few days there was fierce fighting particularly in the south where the Russians were on more equal terms but it was only a question of time before Panzer armour thrust deep into Russian territory.

After breaking through frontier defences and fierce counter attacks, German Panzer Divisions were soon grinding and clanking their way across flat, open countryside. Lacking sufficient heavy tanks, mobile artillery and air support, all that the Russians could do was to bleed the enemy wherever possible by savaging the German armoured columns and mechanized infantry.

The type of action taking place at this time across a broad front is described in Colonel Sharipov's book, *General Chernyakhovsky* — a documentary novel about the youngest commander in the Soviet Army:

'Through a periscope on the tank turret Chernyakhovsky saw a German Panzer-IV hitting a Soviet BT-7 from a distance of some 800 metres. The latter flared up like a torch. He swung the turret and fired but the shell rebounded from the frontal armour of the German tank. Chernyakhovsky was furious: "Oh hell! Our shells can't pierce enemy armour from that distance!"

'He ordered the driver to take the tank toward the enemy lead tank at top speed. At his signal Major Onishchuk's other tanks followed him. Now the enemy tank was only 400 to 500 metres away. Chernyakhovsky was feverishly trying to catch the enemy tank in the gun sights.

'"Fire!" The shell hit the side of the Panzer-IV. The armoured monster which had seemed invulnerable a moment ago, whirled madly round its axis. "Got it!" Ivan shouted in delight to the driver. "Can you see it, Misha? The Nazi is burning! That means we should close the range to knock them out!"'

Later in the action German bombers discovered Chernyakhovsky's armoured division and attacked it: '... Soviet fighters soon appeared over the battlefield. The tankmen were overjoyed. Two Soviet I-16 fighters sat on the tails of the German bombers and forced them to retreat. Suddenly, a Messerschmitt dived out of the clouds above and swooped down on one of the Soviet fighters. A streak of tracer bullets caught it in full view of the tankmen, and it plummeted to the ground, leaving a trail of smoke behind. The explosion set fire to a wheat field. The smoke smarted the eyes. Chernyakhovsky watched in anguish, the other Soviet fighter, which was slower than its foe, catching fire, too. "What's that? Our tanks and planes burn like matches!" somebody said. Chernyakhovsky kept silent.

'As an armoured division commander he was informed that the Red Army had new T-34 and KV tanks, which were the best in the world. They had more powerful engines, larger-calibre guns and thicker armour. Under the mobilization plan one of the regiments of his division was to be equipped with T-34 and KV tanks in July 1941. The war, however, disrupted this plan. On the eve of the war the Red Army had only received about 1,300 T-34s and some 500 KVs. The Air Force did not fare much better. The number of up-to-date Yak and MiG fighters was under 2,000 and that of dive bombers, 500. The German army had half as many again modern tanks and three times as many aircraft. It was vital for the Soviet Union to gain time and re-equip its armed forces. This, however, could not have been done.'

Field actions like this must have been going on all across the battle line as the Germans advanced. The two I-16 Russian aircraft involved were 'Ratas' — the slow, older generation of chunky, radial engined fighters. Some 250 of them had been lost in the Spanish Civil War and they were no match for an Me 109. The tank action, vividly described by Colonel Sharipov, demonstrates how quickly Russian tank commanders learned to manoeuvre their lighter tanks and get within close range in order to knock out German Panzers. But it is apparent even in this short extract that Russia wasn't equipped either in the air or on the ground to contain German armoured thrusts.

By 24 June, 48 hours after the invasion began, German divisions were well into Russian-annexed Poland and the Baltic States, occupying Brest-Litovsk, Vilna and Kovno and were breaking through on other fronts. The Luftwaffe had control of the air and had virtually neutralized the Red Air Force. On 1 July the Germans had taken Riga and forward units were on the banks of the Beresina river. It began to look to the outside world as if a German victory was well within Hitler's grasp. Even Winston

Churchill — after studying all his intelligence reports, maps and statistics of the battle scene — considered that the war could be over in two months and that the Germans might well attempt an invasion of Britain in September or October.

All this made it very difficult for Churchill to decide what help he could give to the Soviets. The attack on Russia had given the war a new dimension with global implications as far as British strategic policies were concerned. One of the first actions to be taken by the British to help Russia was to step up daylight fighter sorties over Northern France to force the Luftwaffe to bring back some of its air power to the Western Front. In addition, both day and night bombing raids on selective targets were intensified.

From the outset, Stalin had been requesting aid and as the Russians were forced to retreat he made it clear that he expected Britain, as an ally, to open up a second front in Europe and the Arctic simultaneously. Churchill quickly reminded him that the Germans had forty divisions in France alone and that the entire coastal area of Northern France was an arsenal of guns and fortifications; also, that Britain had been fighting alone for a year and its current resources were stretched to the limit.

In his initial dialogue with Stalin, Churchill could only basically give him moral support and encouragement stressing the air strikes which were taking place and possible future Naval operations in the Arctic. Britain, heavily committed in the Middle East and other areas was in no position to mount any major offensive action and Churchill was desperately playing for time. He had been putting the utmost pressure on the Americans, who still hadn't come into the war, for an immediate increase of aid of all kinds and especially tanks and guns.

On 12 July, almost three weeks after Germany had invaded, an Anglo-Soviet agreement was signed in Moscow in which Britain and Russia agreed to join hands in the fight against Germany and make no separate peace treaty with the common enemy. By mid-July most of Smolensk was in German hands and a fierce battle was raging in the northern part of the city, but encircled Russian armies would not surrender and carried on fighting for another ten days. The scale of the assault and the street fighting that ensued can be gauged by the fact that the German High Command admitted that about a quarter of a million men were lost at Smolensk.

The Russians were retreating on all fronts and the Soviet leader was pressurizing Churchill for aid which could not be supplied:

3,000 fighters and bombers, thousands of anti-aircraft guns, flame throwers, heavy bombs as well as details and specimens of night fighting equipment and airborne radar. Raw materials requested included rubber, tin, wool, jute, lead, shellac and in addition Stalin wanted millions of pairs of ankle boots and woollen clothes. Churchill warned him that all this was going to take time but not to hesitate about making further suggestions for anything he wanted.

In late July, Churchill telegraphed about a possible Naval operation upon German shipping in Northern Norway and Finland and went on to say: 'We are also studying, as a further development, the basing of some British fighter air squadrons on Murmansk. This would require first of all a consignment of anti-aircraft guns, in addition to ground staff and equipment, then the arrival of the aircraft, some of which could be flown off carriers and others crated.'

Churchill was under very great strain at this particular time when he was making promises to Stalin about forthcoming aid and doing his best to encourage the Soviet leader. Simultaneously, he was pointing out the gravity of the Russian situation to President Roosevelt and reminding him that the whole structure and fabric of the free Western world hung precariously in the balance.

American policy makers regarded the Battle of the Atlantic as the major battle upon which Britain should, in their opinion, concentrate all her resources and effort. They were not convinced that British presence in the Middle East was of prime importance especially as this theatre of war soaked up such a large percentage of American war supplies. Criticism of British strategic policy at this juncture was extremely worrying and Churchill and his Chiefs of Staff had great difficulty in winning the Americans over.

There were also problems for Churchill on the domestic front. Some of the war supplies for Russia would come from our factories and British public opinion was dubious about going 'hand in hand' with a Communist regime. Churchill and his war propaganda machine had to mount a national public relations campaign to change attitudes and promote admiration for the Russian struggle against Nazi tyranny. Churchill's oratory backed up by the media did the trick and the Russians became accepted as our allies fighting for a common cause. It was hardly surprising that 'Russian Rose' was to become one of the most popular songs of the times!

In late July, Churchill informed Stalin that the British War

Cabinet had decided to send Hurricane fighters to help the Soviet Air Force and these would be despatched as soon as possible. But, as yet, no British supply convoy had set sail for Russia and it was not until August that the first convoy carrying aid was despatched.

Two days later, Air Chief Marshal Sir Charles Portal went to see Churchill with the Air Ministry's outline plan to send a Hurricane Wing to Murmansk. Portal explained the job that it would have to do in Northern Russia and Churchill told him to proceed at once, saying that we must give what help was possible. As a result of these discussions 151 Wing was born.

Chapter 3
Exeter

504 Squadron said goodbye to Filton in late December 1940 and flew into Exeter where it was to remain for six months or more covering South-west England from 'hit and run raids' and carrying out convoy patrols. Shortly after they arrived, Chan Heywood, who had been flying with Wag Haw during the Battle of Britain was posted. Chan had previously flown Fairey Battles during the fall of France which had been a fairly 'hairy' occupation and was due for a rest. Wag was sorry to see him go after all the 'piss-ups' and fun they had enjoyed together.

Much to Wag's astonishment Ibby Waud suddenly arrived on the scene. There was no mistaking that great hunk of a Yorkshireman when Ibby walked into the Sergeants' Mess took a look around and spotted him. They hadn't seen one another for well over a year, not since the old days at Brough, and had a lot of catching up to do. Ibby didn't say anything about his bad luck at not getting himself on a squadron and missing all the fighting so far. But right from the start when they teamed up at Exeter they formed a rather odd partnership.

Wag, shortish, cobby and ebullient was naive in some ways and his emotions were never far from the surface. Ibby on the other hand, tall and solidly built, was a more sophisticated character rather gruff in manner and not given to outbursts of enthusiasm. Both men were totally dedicated in their desire to become top fighter pilots and it was undoubtedly Ibby's frustration at being out of the action that had led him into trouble with the RAF establishment.

From a flying point of view Wag now had the advantage because he had been with the Squadron for over six months and had gained a great deal of combat experience. Tony Rook, his Flight commander, had become a father figure and taken a personal interest in him. About that time there had been requests for pilots from 504 to be posted to newly-formed squadrons but Tony Rook would not let Sergeant Haw go. Wag had established himself as an outstanding member of the Squadron with great potential.

Ibby Waud was mad keen to get some action but the period at Exeter did not produce many encounters with the enemy. It wasn't until 3 April that he fired his guns in anger for the first time. Tony Rook had recently been promoted to Squadron Leader and had taken over 504. Ibby was flying with Rook and Pilot Officer Hunt on a convoy patrol and the section was patrolling a magnificent line-ahead of warships when the convoy came under attack from a Heinkel. The Hurricanes promptly shot down the Heinkel which flopped quite nicely into the sea, forcing the crew out into a dinghy. In the aftermath Sergeant Pilot Ibby Waud was duly credited with one third of a Hun confirmed.

Another Heinkel which the Squadron shot down had rather different repercussions which affected everybody. Flying Officer Trevor Parsons was leading the section which bagged it. The BBC, in its enthusiasm, broadcast on that particular morning that Hurricanes from Exeter had shot down a Heinkel bomber. The Germans picked up the transmission and that night a Flight of Heinkels came in at low level and plastered the airfield in retaliation.

It happened to be an evening when Wag Haw had run short of booze money and decided that the only thing to do was to nip into the station cinema and see what Betty Grable was up to. In the middle of the programme there was a deafening roar and a series of explosions. The lights went out and the cinema seemed to dance up and down on springs as everybody made for the exits. At Wag's way out people were all in a heap having tripped over a bomb which had failed to explode.

The airfield and buildings were heavily damaged during the raid and Wag and Ibby in company with others had to be billeted out. The pub they used most frequently was the Bowd Inn and it was during the time when Winston Churchill had launched his V for Victory campaign urging people to paint V signs everywhere. Ibby thought that this was a splendid idea and with a pot of paint and a brush from stores enthusiastically covered the local area including the Bowd Inn car park. It was tremendous fun at the time especially as he and Wag were more than slightly 'pissed' but as Ibby said when a chap rushed out of the bar and saw a large V sign on his car door, 'It seems to me Wag, that Devonians don't go along with Winston Churchill over this V sign lark!'

It was in this period that Ibby really learned and enjoyed Squadron formation flying. 'We used to throw the formations all over the sky', he said, 'and sometimes when Wag and I went up together we performed semi-aerobatic formation flying — enormous stall turns were our speciality.'

Wag Haw found convoy patrols to be rather boring affairs and reckoned at one stage that he knew the names of every boat that left Brixham Harbour. On his way down to the coast he used to do aerobatics before having to fly round and round a convoy at about 1,000 ft, first one way and then the other. It seemed to him at the time that it was rather a stupid business because German aircraft made lightning attacks at low level and his Hurricane didn't stand a chance in hell of catching the bastards!

While sitting around in Flights one day the news came through that a barrage balloon had broken loose and was wallowing about like a drunken sailor near the coast on the outskirts of Plymouth. The voice on the field telephone asked if a Squadron Hurricane could whizz over and shoot it down. Wag immediately volunteered and ran out to his aircraft before anybody else could stake a prior claim.

It was a perfect day for having a bit of sport up in the clouds and the thought of shooting up a barrage balloon in Wag's mind conjured up images of the Western Front in World War 1 when German observation balloons were prime targets. He was excited as he opened the throttle wide and climbed furiously with his nose pointing high into the heavens.

Great dollops of cumulus cloud looking like pyramids of ice cream sparkled in the sun as they sailed along the coast like a great armada. With fingers gently caressing the stick and a hand resting lightly on the throttle he could feel the power and reverberations of his Merlin engine going through his body like electric impulses as his Hurricane clawed its way up the sides of mountains of swirling cloud.

The cockpit was warm and comfortable and glancing back he could see his aircraft silhouetted against the cloud and moving with him like some ghostly shadow. He levelled out at 12,000 ft, throttling back and gently weaving the aircraft to take a closer look at the frothy mattress of cloud formations down below, which resembled an Arctic landscape. Tightening his harness straps, he stood the Hurricane on its tail, kicking on rudder and letting the nose fall out of the sky in a stall turn. The cumulus peaks rushed up into his windscreen as he slid down the clouds and pulled back on the stick feeling the force of gravity weighing him down as he shot upwards blinking into the sun. Then he looped and rolled, coming down like a falling leaf twisting and turning, throwing his aircraft around the sky in a state of wild abandon challenging the Hurricane by flying closer and closer to the stall. Feeling her shudder and shake before he let her free to fly and then pushing her again and again to the limit knowing that he was the master and feeling good about it.

It seemed a pity to break away from those minutes of ecstasy in a revolving world of fermentations of moisture and fantasy. Testing out his Hurricane in the great dimensions of the sky always made him feel like a small boy with the key to the universe in his hands.

Diving through a gap in the sporting clouds he gave Plymouth a wide berth and south of the moors caught a glimpse of his quarry highlighted in the sun. A great big blown up sausage-like monster trailing wires in the wind and floating gently towards the coast in the direction of Start Point. He headed towards it and roared past, taking a closer look at the wires before making a wide turn, switching on his gunsight and firing button thinking that this was all going to be terrific fun.

He supposed that when he pumped lead into it the whole thing would go up in flames as the observation balloons had done in the old war films. He could picture the observer rolling out of his underslung basket and parachuting down to earth in a frenzy. As he came round and lined up the balloon in his gunsight he felt that he really was Biggles on the Western Front flying his SE 5. It made him realize that they were all Biggles at heart, Ibby Waud, the Royces, the Rooks, in fact the whole damned lot of them.

When he opened fire he could feel his wings vibrating and knew that he was punching holes in the great big old grey bag. He flashed past skimming the top and turned to see what had happened, but the balloon seemed untouched and was still floating merrily along. He came in even closer on his second attack and poured lead into it but with no effect as far as he could make out. The thought that he couldn't even shoot down a defenceless balloon was beginning to irritate him because he knew what the boys would say when he got back. Finally he ran out of ammunition and had to leave his quarry floating out to sea and looking untouched. He really couldn't understand it because he knew that he must have drilled lots of holes into the bloody fabric but the damned thing had got the better of him and he felt that he should have got out and kicked it to death. They told him later that the balloon had finally come down in the sea about ten miles off the coast, but the laugh was on him.

Escorting bombers was more fun than anything else and 504 provided top cover on several occasions to Blenheims which were bombing specific targets in Northern France. Watching bombs burst on the quay at Le Havre was more exciting than flying round and round convoys and the Squadron was itching to get more action.

Shortly after Hitler invaded Russia Fighter Command's air war was stepped up across the Channel with more fighter sweeps and bomber escorts. These activities were carried out in an attempt to force the Luftwaffe to divert aircraft from the Russian front. But 504 was not a front line offensive squadron and had to be satisfied with an occasional chance to 'have a go' over Northern France.

In mid-July the commanding officer, Tony Rook, announced that the Squadron was to fly to Fairwood Common to do a conversion course on to the new Hurricane Mark IIC equipped with 20mm cannons. The new machines, he said in his quiet and rather matter of fact way, would enable the Squadron to go over on the offensive and get plenty of action on the other side of the Channel. This was the news that everybody had been waiting for. Tony Rook was a popular chap having recently taken over from Johnny Sample, who had led the Squadron before the fall of France. His appearance suggested a rather stagey type since he was over six feet with a large up-twirling black moustache and longish black hair. He was a cinema screen version of what most people thought a fighter pilot should look like including the firm and resolute jaw. Rook was also well spoken with a deep voice: relaxed and totally unflappable, he had the manner to go with it. The family business Skinner and Rook, who were wine merchants in Nottingham, was a marvellous springboard for joining the local Auxiliary squadron — which happened to be 504!

His cousin Micky commanded 'A' Flight on his squadron and made a point of calling him 'Sir' in the Mess. Micky was even taller, being 6 ft 4 in, and temperamentally quite different. Unlike his cousin, Micky was a 'nice flapper' in the most charming and kindly way. The two combined to make a great team in a squadron which had operated in a family atmosphere since it became a fighter squadron at Hucknall on 31 October 1938. The Squadron flew into Fairwood Common, an airfield on the outskirts of Swansea, on 21 July 1941. Three days later it provided second cover wing for bombers returning from Brest. This was the largest daylight offensive operation carried out to date and 129 bombers took part including Wellingtons, Hampdens, Fortresses and Halifaxes. Life was getting more interesting for all concerned, but before pilots had a chance of flying their new machines something suddenly happened which was to change the entire structure of 504 Auxiliary Fighter Squadron.

Wag Haw had gone off to air test his machine and, as always, he took the opportunity of doing some aerobatics and generally playing around and having fun in the sky. On this particular morning he was flying at 5,000 ft and decided to have a go at an 'Upavon Twizzle' a specialist aerobatic in which the pilot had to try to get his aircraft to spin around its propeller. The idea being to stand the aircraft on its tail near the stall, pull back on the stick and apply full rudder as for a flick roll — and then pray.

The 'Upavon Twizzle' wasn't exactly an authorized aerobatic because it put a great deal of strain upon the fan up front and the tail assembly. Apart from that a pilot could get into all kinds of trouble hanging suspended by his prop and sliding backwards on his tailplane. Trevor Parsons had tried it once at Filton when he was rather low and the fan had stopped at the *'moment critique'*. Trevor had been terribly lucky to get the machine under control and down in one piece with a dead prop. Inevitably, he collected a well-deserved rocket from his CO, Johnny Sample, who had witnessed the aerial display through his telescope!

It was always a challenge for any pilot to 'have a go' at this particular stunt and Wag was determined to do more revolutions around his propeller than anybody else. On this particular morning Wag did a half roll and dived steeply, pulling his stick back and climbing as near vertically as possible at full throttle. It was an unnatural feeling for a pilot to sit back in his seat and stare into the sky waiting for his aircraft to lose flying speed while his controls went limp and the machine began to shudder and shake as if it was having convulsions.

Wag waited until the last second before his Hurricane would slide backwards out of control and then, sensing the moment, he pulled the stick back and applied rudder. She did three turns around the prop shaking and vibrating like hell before the nose fell

Above *A Vic formation of Hurricanes flies over dispersals at Vianga.*

Below *Before the onset of winter, a solo Hurricane beats up the airfield.*

Left *81 Squadron outside the Flight hut. Squadron Leader Tony Rook is seated third from the left. Flight Sergeant Wag Haw stands on the extreme right.*

Below left *By the tail of his Hurricane and under the watchful gaze of a Russian soldier, the diminutive Flight Lieutenant Ross unbuckles his parachute after a sortie.*

Right *The grave of Sergeant 'Nudger' Smith on a small rise overlooking Murmansk Sound.*

Below *A frequent routine on the airfield — the pumping out of lakes formed at dispersals!*

Above *Pilots of 134 Squadron posing outside their partially dug-out Flight hut.*

Below *From the airfield, the silhouette of a silver birch tree stands out against a background of combat vapour trails.*

away and the world turned upside down. It was like doing a flick roll in a vertical position going backwards and Wag was relieved when his Hurricane decided that enough was enough because he was ready to 'chicken out' at the time.

When he got back to base Corporal Dixon who looked after 'Flights' told him that the CO, Tony Rook, wanted to see him and he immediately thought that he was going to get a rocket for performing the 'Upavon Twizzle'. When he walked into the hut everybody was gathered there and Tony Rook announced that 'A' Flight was to be transferred to 81 Squadron and that a new 504 was to be built up from 'B' Flight. Furthermore, the CO said that he would be taking over 81 Squadron which was to be posted overseas.

This was major surgery as far as 504 was concerned and it came as quite a surprise. Most people had realized that the RAF was poised for rapid expansion and that squadrons were bound to be broken up to form new units. 504 had been lucky to remain intact for so long. At least, Wag thought, Tony and Micky Rook would keep the old 504 spirit alive in the new squadron leaving people like Jo and 'Scruffy' Royce from 'B' Flight to rebuild the old one.

The whole of 'A' Flight were immediately sent on leave and ordered to report back to Leconfield — a fighter station in Yorkshire. Nobody knew where they were going to be posted except that it was somewhere overseas.

Chapter 4
Assembly for Russia

On their way home to York on leave Wag and Ibby discussed where they might land up overseas. Both agreed that there wouldn't be much action at home until the big fighter sweeps and bomber escort work really got going. They hadn't fired their guns much over the past few months and Ibby was still binding away at having missed the big air battles.

Wag pointed out that the only real action to be had at the moment was in Russia. 'There's little doing in the Middle East' he said, 'except armies running around the desert going forwards and backwards as far as I can make out. I think you'll find, Ibby, that we might possibly land up in Russia the way things are looking.' Ibby thought for a moment, 'You could be right, Wag you know.' He scratched his forehead, contemplating the thought, and grunted, 'Bloody good show then — the sooner the better for me.'

When they reported to Leconfield after leave it was a question of finding the location of 81 Squadron, 151 Wing. The fighter station was a big one housing Czech, Polish and English fighter squadrons and there were the usual well established Messes, acres of barrack blocks, stores buildings, hangars and a vast airfield which seemed to stretch into infinity. Eventually they were told to make their way round the perimeter and they would find the Expedition headquarters in a crew room on the far side of the airfield.

There they were glad to see some familiar faces and felt good to be back with the chaps again. A lot of wisecracking and fooling about was going on, with the boys swapping stories of piss-ups and parties during leave. Wag caught sight of the newly-promoted Pilot Officers Artie Holmes and Bas Bush in serious discussion in one corner and gave them a two-fingered salute — it was Artie who had baled out and landed in a dustbin outside Victoria Station and Bas who had his windscreen shattered by a shell during the Battle of Britain.

The Canadians Jimmy Walker and Dave Ramsey were sitting outside with their backs to the wall taking in the sun and looking rather bored with life. The Commanding Officer, Tony Rook, was chalking names on a blackboard with his cousin Micky Rook and McGregor looking on. It looked as if everybody was hanging around so Wag and Ibby joined the other NCOs including Avro Anson, and Nudger Smith who were standing in a group. Nudger introduced them to a new face by the name of Ginger Carter who asked Wag why the boys called Smith 'Nudger'. Wag winked and told him that Smith swore that if ever he got shot down and got the chop he would come back and 'nudge' the lads.

The pilots were bored with having to hang about and wanted to know what was going on or, in their language, 'what the form was' and the bets were on the Middle East because there weren't many other places where they could be posted. It was some time before they were all called together and addressed by a Wing Commander rejoicing in the name of Ramsbottom Isherwood who told them that he had taken command of 151 Wing and that they would shortly be sailing for Murmansk, a port on the tip of Northern Russia.

Everything went quiet for a second or two and then there were gasps and whistles and a buzz of conversation. Wag heard Jimmy Walker, the Canadian, exclaim, 'Jeesus Cheerist', which just about summed it up. Not that anybody was other than keen to go to Russia because that was where the action was and it would be an adventure — something that they could look back on all their lives — but the news that they were going somewhere on the edge of the Arctic Circle was a bit difficult to take in all at once.

A few chuckles went round on the subject of the Wing Commander's name, Ramsbottom Isherwood, which sounded a bit odd. But there was nothing like that about the tough and wiry little New Zealander. He was in his mid-thirties, grey haired with a hard mouth and chin and immediately gave the impression of a man not to be trifled with. His DFC and AFC were symbols of his courage in combat and also as a test pilot of long experience. He had put in more flying hours than any of them and as far as young pilots were concerned Wing Commander was a very dizzy rank. They listened attentively to his short speech welcoming them to the Wing and watched him retreat into the background after he had handed over to his aides.

Basically they were only interested in their aeroplanes and what they had to do in the air. All the other detail and paraphernalia surrounding their lives was incidental. They relied totally on the RAF to look after them in that respect because flying was the only thing that mattered.

Having had their inoculations and attended a few lectures the pilots were sent on leave again because there was nothing for them to do and it was going to take some time before the Expedition was ready to go. Wag Haw had a nasty moment when the Medical Officer stuck a needle in his arm, causing him to faint and there was a discussion as to whether he was fit enough to go to Russia!

There was one man in the Wing who knew quite a lot about Russia having been there on several occasions pre-war and he even spoke the language. His name was Hubert Griffith and he was a Flight Lieutenant who was posted to 151 as Wing Adjutant. When the Germans invaded Russia and the Soviets became our ally, Griff had immediately asked the Air Ministry to be sent to Russia in any capacity. At the beginning of August he received a telegram while on leave telling him to report to No 151 Fighter Wing forthwith and take over the Adjutant role. No mention was made of Russia and he telephoned his station, which was a Recruits Training Centre in Lancashire, to find out more about it. He was told that the whole thing was 'hush-hush' but his posting was probably the job he had asked for.

Griff had spent the best part of a year in a parade ground existence of button-cleaning and drill. When he arrived at Leconfield he told a chum that 'it is like a month's holiday even to be in the atmosphere of an operational station again'. He found life on a fighter station to be an uplifting and challenging experience after months of Training Command. A place without 'bullshit' where everyone got on with the job in a most direct and informal way.

It was, in his own words, 'like a dream of heaven' after a strict disciplinarian routine but there was more to it than that. He felt himself to be part of a machine which was in direct contact with the war as he watched Hurricanes and Spitfires roaring through the air and smelt the mixture of petrol and engine oil which pervaded hangars crowded with mechanics servicing the fighters.

There was something quite different about being on an operational station. He could see, hear and smell it. It wasn't simply the informality of daily life or the sense of purpose in everybody going about their daily tasks which roused him. As an administrator or 'wingless wonder' he always found excitement in new surroundings, but suddenly being pitchforked into Leconfield was like being catapulted from base camp into the front line and he loved it.

Flight Lieutenant Hubert Griffith found himself totally immersed in the formation of the new Wing right from the start because when he arrived most people were either on leave or about to go. The CO, Ramsbottom Isherwood, the Squadron Leader (Admin), clerical staff, airmen, all the pilots and the two squadron commanders, Tony Rook and Tony Miller had all gone. One of his first jobs was to get the remainder of the 550 men who were going to Russia off as well. There was a stack of paperwork because they all had to have three official documents signed by an officer including leave-passes, railway-warrants and ration cards.

Before the men started trickling back he was able to watch fighter pilots from the resident squadrons 'off duty' in the Mess and was surprised how quiet they were. Nobody seemed to talk or get excited about the day's 'ops' not even when one of the squadrons had shot down a Ju 88 while on patrol over the North Sea. Griff only got to hear about it later that evening in the Mess when the Squadron Intelligence officer concerned was telling people that he got the combat story of the action through to Fighter Command within fifteen minutes after de-briefing the pilot and had expected a pat on the back. But Fighter Command didn't think this was quick enough and told him so. Hence he was 'having a go' at Fighter Command, otherwise Griff would have known nothing about the Ju 88.

He had rather expected that there would have been some sort of celebration in the Mess that evening but nothing happened and nobody else mentioned anything about 'bagging a Hun'. Griff didn't know at the time that pilots' parties just get going when the boys are in the mood and often for no particular reason but he was to find out as time went on.

As the Wing reassembled after leave Air Ministry signals continued to come in regarding additional postings and Griffith records some of these in his diary. 'Air Ministry to Sutton Valence: Despatch immediately by road to Peake Moor (Leconfield) two Sergeant Pilots complete with parachutes, Mae Wests and dinghies.' 'From Sutton Valence to Air Ministry: Two Sergeant Pilots with parachutes, Mae Wests and dinghies despatched by road 28-7-41.' And yet another signal to confirm that the Sergeant Pilots had actually been despatched and so it went on day after day. It all sounded rather bizarre, as if Sergeant Pilots were like cattle yet had to have their parachutes in case they fell out of the lorry!

One of the big problems at this stage was to keep people occupied because there was little for them to do except to check kit, attend the odd lecture and hang around. The pilots, who were quite capable of getting into all sorts of trouble, were sent on leave again — they hadn't got any aeroplanes to fly and could well have been a disturbing influence on the resident squadrons who were operational.

The Wing Adjutant, Hubert Griffith, was well aware that getting an RAF Wing on the road was a complex and highly skilled business. The Wing Headquarters Unit alone comprised some 350 personnel including medical, equipment, signals, engineering, maintenance, transport and non-technical staff who provided the labour force. The two Squadrons, nos 81 and 134, each had their own Squadron and Flight commanders plus thirty or more pilots and a back-up of about a hundred airmen to keep them in the air.

Only the officers and non-commissioned pilots knew that the Wing was going to Russia and they were told not to mention anything. Despite these precautions there was soon a general rumour going around that everybody was destined for a place called Murmansk but as nobody had ever heard of Murmansk they regarded the loose talk as 'duff gen'. As far as they were concerned they might just as well be going to Tipperary or up the Nile because there was nothing that they could do about it, so why bother?

On one particular Friday when 151 Wing pilots had returned from leave, Hubert Griffith recorded in his diary that a rather super party developed in the Mess late in the evening. The resident squadrons had shot down two Huns during the day and that was a good enough reason for the chaps to be in the mood. One of these squadrons happened to be Czech with a few English officers and some Poles who had been in residence for some time. Usually these occasions materialized without preconception and for that reason were tremendous fun. A Czech Squadron Leader who could accompany anything on his violin added to the quality of the singing by keeping the chaps more or less in tune. Anybody who could make music, like Wag Haw on his piano, was invaluable on these occasions. The party was generally building up with the booze flowing and songs orchestrated when at about 11.00 pm the entire show was quite suddenly and spontaneously transformed. The Czechoslovakian fiddle had been livening everybody up with Russian peasant music. Instinctively, the chaps took off their tunics and collars, pulled out their shirts and tied their ties around their waists. On the spur of the moment everyone became a Russian 'muzhik', singing, dancing and clapping hands around the Czech fiddler. It was an explosion of fun and good feeling between the resident pilots and those who had just dropped in on their way to the Arctic.

The climax of the evening came when Flight Lieutenant Ross of 134 Squadron was lifted up on to the large tall mantelpiece in the ante-room. He must have been the smallest pilot ever to have flown a Hurricane, being only a little over 4 ft tall and perched up there on the mantelpiece he could neither get up nor down. He was compelled to remain up there and make a speech to the riotous assembly, which he carried out with remarkable composure and skill as if he had been making speeches from mantelpieces all his life.

Meanwhile Ramsbottom Isherwood and his staff had only one object in mind and that was to get the expedition off as quickly as possible because with one delay after another it was becoming increasingly difficult to keep people occupied. One Saturday morning when the entire Wing — except for one man who had absconded while on leave — was re-assembled Hubert Griffith had a bright idea and suggested to Isherwood that a small route march might help to keep the chaps fit before the long sea journey. The Wing Commander thought this was a splendid idea and gave instructions that everybody, including pilots, should take part.

Walking through Yorkshire lanes and across moors was not an occupation which appealed to Hurricane pilots who thought that the 'Wing Adj' should take a 'running jump' but they went off just the same, grousing and grumbling. The New Zealand Wing Commander, had not minced his words and was certainly not a man to argue with. Although he enjoyed a joke, he was a stern character and, as Hubert Griffith said, 'he had a mouth like a rat trap'.

During this period of delays there was a lot of talking behind closed doors and sometimes the chaps got the impression that the expedition would never 'get off the ground'. The non-commissioned pilots felt quite strongly that they were not being given the 'gen' and only the officers knew what was going on. They felt, not unnaturally, that they were on the outside of the circle. As Wag Haw said, 'nobody ever tells us what's going on, the officers know far more about it than we do — we're only Sergeant Pilots'.

These sentiments expressed by Wag were only 'niggles' which surfaced when the boys got frustrated by having little to do except hang about. But there was a very real concern amongst a number of Sergeant Pilots about being non-commissioned and having to fly across the Channel over enemy territory. Ibby Waud who had strong 'Ibby-ish' views on the matter felt that any fighter pilot having to come down in enemy territory should at least be afforded officer rank and treatment in a prisoner-of-war camp.

Most of this was just talk and no Sergeant Pilot was prepared to stand up and make an issue out of it although there was some justification for Ibby's view. Their overriding passion in life was the excitement of flying and fighting and for them nothing else really mattered.

Just when it seemed that the Expedition would have to be 'aborted' because of the continual delays and the approach of a Russian winter the news at last came through that they were to move out. At 5.30 am on a Monday morning of mid-August the Advance Party comprising 23 airmen and led by Flight Lieutenants Rook and Cottam piled into trucks and departed. Hubert Griffith wrote in his diary, 'I get up in the dews of dawn to see them off and they all seem in good form. Our turn, that of the Main Party, is to come tonight'.

Roll call and check-out for the Wing was conducted at 18.00 hours in the large number one hanger with everybody in cheerful mood and only anxious to get on with it. As most of them had no idea where they were actually going except 'some place overseas' there was a good deal of guesswork but it wasn't until their civvy packet boat had left Liverpool and was well out to sea that they were told they were on their way to Russia!

The Hurricane pilots of both Squadrons had been sent on leave for the third time and when they returned to Leconfield the Wing had departed. Both Wag Haw and Ibby Waud, who couldn't face going back to York yet again, spent their extra few days leave in a splendid pub in Scarborough having a last fling. Soon after they got back movement instructions came through and they climbed aboard a rather ancient Handley Page Harrow with a high wing and fixed undercarriage and were flown to Abbotsinch on the outskirts of Glasgow. Then they were conveyed by truck to Gourock and boarded HMS *Argus*, which set sail for Scapa Flow. 151 Wing had finally left Leconfield in the hands of the resident Squadrons who carried on with the job of shooting down any Hun who had the temerity to poke his nose into their particular territory of ocean expanse. Life finally returned to a degree of normality on the huge airfield and the English, Czech and Polish pilots in the Officers' Mess wondered now and again how those poor bastards going to Russia were getting on. The piss-ups and the parties they all enjoyed were a fading memory and only the junk left behind in number one hangar was reminder that 151 Wing had ever existed.

Chapter 5
Heading North

During the last two weeks in August while 151 Wing was sailing towards Murmansk the airmen on board the convoy were blissfully unaware that the war had taken a dramatic turn and Hitler appeared to be in sight of victory. Soviet troops had evacuated Novgorod which was only about a hundred miles south of Leningrad and in the south the German army was closing in on the Caucasus. Towards the end of the month the giant dam on the Dnieper at Zaporozhe was blown up pending the arrival of German forces and the Ukrainian industrial centre of Dnepropetrovsk had been evacuated.

In the far northern tundra area surrounding Murmansk General Dietl's Mountain Jägers were preparing to mount a final onslaught on Murmansk and his Mountain Corps had been reinforced with two regiments — the 9th SS 'Death's Head' Infantry Regiment and the 388th Infantry Regiment. Hitler's original plan to cut the Murmansk railway line in the region of Kandalaksha some 220 miles further south and also at Loukhi about ninety miles or more further on, got bogged down with German divisions stuck in the terrain short of their objectives.

Everything depended on the success of 'Operation Platinum Fox' which was the name given to the advance on Murmansk itself. The German High Command which had been enjoying successes along a front which stretched for almost 1,500 miles would not accept that operations in Northern Russia were not proceeding according to plan. Hence Dietl was given reinforcements to force his way through to the road to Murmansk. The initial phase of the campaign had gone well. Dietl's Mountain divisions had blocked the Rybachiy or Fisherman's Island as it was called, and headed towards the road to Murmansk. They took the Titovka bridge and crossed the river. The Soviet army camp on the far side was deserted and so was the airfield but where they had expected to find a road leading towards Litsa and on to Murmansk there was nothing but routes of telephone lines and the tracks where nomadic Lapps had crossed the tundra.

Finnish intelligence, upon which the Germans had relied, had assumed that dotted lines on the maps represented paths or roads where in fact they only denoted lines of telegraph posts. German forward units were then confronted with outlying Russian defences consisting of pill boxes in rough terrain but with no supply routes to back them up. The pill boxes were manned by Siberian and Mongolian troops who fought to the death. They would not be flushed out either with flame throwers or grenades and the mountain troops had to by-pass them leaving it to the Luftwaffe and artillery to blast them out.

This fierce close fighting was going on during the height of a Russian summer but Dietl had to drive hard for every inch of ground knowing that his Labour Service men were stretched to the limit in building supply routes behind him. He was fighting a brutal and bloody battle in a pathless country searching for the road to Murmansk which was rapidly becoming a fantasy.

Time and again during the slog towards Murmansk he must have remembered his Führer's words, 'You've got to manage those ridiculous sixty miles from Petsamo to Murmansk with your Mountain Jägers'. When his 137th Mountain Regiment suddenly came upon a deserted area and found supplies of food and over one hundred trucks he knew that he had struck gold. If there were trucks then there must be a road, he thought, and looking down below into the valley he saw a superb modern road carving its way through the rock and scrub. After all the fierce fighting since the invasion began he knew that at last he was within an arm's length of the gateway into Murmansk and 'Operation Platinum Fox', mounted to capture the harbour and cut the Russian supplies rail link, was on the brink of success. He stood there confident that the Russians would not be able to stop him once he got rolling down that road. But first he had to reach it and he had no doubts that his men would have to fight every inch of the way.

* * *

When Flight Sergeant George 'Micky' Turner first heard that he was heading for Northern Russia he reckoned that the civvy packet ship must be at least 100 miles out of Liverpool. He was told that there were about thirty ships in the convoy which was being escorted by the cruiser, HMS *Sheffield* and the destroyer, HMS *Electra*. Not that he worried because they had excellent accommodation with stewards and a jolly good cuisine. Their boat, the *Llanstephan Castle*, a liner of some 20,000 tons, had previously called in to Cape Town for re-victualling and had picked up delicacies which had been scarce or unknown in England for a year or more. There had been a few wise-cracks at first when the boys sat down to breakfast facing a choice of a half-dozen dishes including grapefruit, jam, butter, eggs and bacon. Comments like, 'They'll never believe me when I tell 'em back home', 'Cor, this is the life this is', 'Better than your old egg-powder, eh chum?', 'When did you last see an orange, Taff?' were all part of the general reaction after the shortages in the Old Country.

The boat had been only partially converted into a troopship and life on board carried on in the atmosphere of a luxury cruise liner especially as deck games, evening concerts and 'Housey-Housey' were all part of the itinerary. There were no chores except for the occasional routine inspections, plenty to eat and drink plus fun and games to while away the time.

Like some of the others, Micky Turner's reaction to the Russian business was very positive indeed although a little tempered perhaps with the excellent cuisine aboard ship. He looked at it as something different, something new in the sense that many times during his RAF career he had wished that something exceptional would happen — and now it had. It was all going to be a great adventure, he thought, and he was damned lucky to get the chance.

He couldn't help thinking like that because he had been in the RAF since he had joined in 1930 as a boy apprentice at Halton or a 'Trenchard brat' as they were known. It seemed a long time ago now as he sat out in the sun mesmerized by the white foamy wash looking like a boiling cauldron of soapsuds as it rushed along the side of the ship. Three years of slog finishing up with one and sixpence a day as a 'fitter, aero engine' but it was worth it. He knew his stuff all right and nobody could take that away from him.

It made him smile thinking back over those years. There they were, 2,700 mischievous boys in a place that resembled a prison camp and all bent on trying to beat the system, breaking out of camp and breaking back in again, marching to workshops and school during the five-day week and wearing a yellow band on the right arm at all times as a badge of distinction.

Looking out to sea reminded him of another boat which he and a chum had just managed to catch by the skin of their teeth when they had escaped from France. It was after Dunkirk and they were making for the port of St Malô taking what transports they could lay hands on. The roads had been packed with refugees and anything could be obtained in exchange for petrol. Some of the spare pilots on the Squadron had hitched a ride in Hurricanes by sitting on the bare pilot's seat while the pilot, minus chute, sat on top of him and flew the Hurricane back to the UK.

Everyone had to forage for himself but one day a Salvation Army canteen appeared out of nowhere with all sorts of 'eats'. It was staffed by two ladies who gave the impression that they were on a Sunday School picnic — so calm, so cool, so nice. On arrival at St Malô he saw lines and lines of trucks, pick-ups and staff cars in a compound all intact. Rather than let the Germans grab them he and his chum set about creating mayhem amongst the machinery or in other words 'they had a ball'. He drove a four-wheel drive Crossley in auxiliary low gear into a line of staff cars resulting in one car riding up on the other until he had them in battered condition up on their ends or turned over. Then he and his chum raced down to the docks to see their boat, which was the last one out, starting to pull away from the jetty and turning round to sail out of the harbour. There was only one thing to do so they took a flying leap and hoped for the best — they just made it and the lads grabbed them and hauled them aboard.

Getting away from France had been an exciting episode but he regarded the prospect of going to Arctic Russia as an adventure which would transcend everything else he had ever done. After they had got the news that they were going to a place called Murmansk, which as far as he could make out was so far north that it was on the edge of the world, he couldn't stop thinking about it. That he was on his way to teach the Russkies how to service and maintain a Hurricane seemed ludicrous at times and the boys had joked about it, creating visions of seductive Russian interpretesses bending over a Merlin engine with notebook and pencil made them all laugh and he sometimes wondered whether it might not be far from the truth. He was soon going to find out!

Any romantic visions that Russia was some sort of earthly paradise were soon shattered by the Wing Adjutant, Hubert Griffith, who gave them a lecture on the subject. Everybody listened intently to Griffith's every word because he was 'a gen man' on Russia and they were all going there. He began by telling them that 99 per cent of everything that they had read about Russia was either biased or exaggerated. His theme was that up to 25 years ago — just a single generation — Russia was the most backward country in Europe by some two or three hundred years and he gave his audience a brief historical analysis of illiterate, peasant Russia.

He then pointed out that, 'It is obvious that there has been an enormous advance, almost inconceivable in its power and speed and wide scope, in the last quarter of a century. We are now going to a country that is so industrialized and organized and educated that it has been able to put into the field an Army that fights on equal terms with Hitler — the only army in Europe that has been able to do this'.

When Hubert Griffith talked about where they were all going and what they were likely to find when the got there he didn't mince his words, 'If by any chance', he said, 'you have read papers, and seen pictures, dealing with modern Russian architecture, culture, science, beauty, leisure — forget it! With regard to where we are going, it is possible that we will have a camp of wooden huts, set down in a mud-flat — and seeing the geographical situation that we will be in, we will have to grin and pretend that we like it.'

Sailing with the Main Party on the *Llanstephan Castle* were some fourteen pilots including Sergeants Eric 'Ginger' Carter and his chum John Mulroy, who had joined Wag Haw and the boys at Leconfield two weeks previously. Both pilots were posted from 615 Squadron to the newly formed 151 Wing and had been flying Hurricanes with 615 Squadron based on Anglesey. For the past few months they had been carrying out convoy and shipping patrols over the Irish Sea and had seen little or no action.

They had had one frustrating experience when they were posted on a night flying course with 456 Squadron which was then being formed as a night-fighter unit. Both men had been rated 'above average' as fighter pilots in their log books but neither wanted to become a night fighter pilot so they did all they could to fail the course. They succeeded in getting themselves posted back to 615 which was still carrying out convoy patrols and when their Squadron Commander, Squadron Leader Powell-Shedden, asked for two volunteers to join a fighter squadron shortly to be posted overseas they duly obliged.

Eric Carter was known as 'Ginger' from the days when he went to Kings Norton Grammar School in Birmingham because he had brilliant wavy red hair. His father wanted him to be a works accountant and he started learning the profession only to find life incredibly boring. He could see no sense in sticking in an office waiting for his call-up papers so he volunteered for the RAFVR to become a fighter pilot. Like the others, Ginger was mad keen on flying, which apart from anything else would give him his freedom and keep him away from petty discipline.

Like Wag Haw and Ibby Waud, Ginger and John Mulroy formed a partnership described in Ginger's words, 'I'll promise to look after your back John and you look after mine.' At first, they thought they might be going to the Middle East but when they were kitted out with heavy leather fur-lined flying jackets and tougher flying boots they felt that it must be somewhere cold and it could be Norway. Upon learning that their destination was up in the Arctic Circle in Northern Russia Ginger said quite simply, 'well, I suppose that it's somewhere to go — somewhere different, I mean. We might never have the chance of going there again!'

As the *Llanstephan Castle* steamed further and further north in the direction of Spitzbergen the crew began to take samples of the sea to check the ice content and it was not long before icebergs began to appear. During this time in August the sun never seemed to set. It dipped down below the horizon at midnight and half-an-hour later the rim slowly reappeared, dispersing a night that never was. The scenario of sun's rays playing on an endless sea broken only by icebergs and schools of spouting whales made the war seem a million miles away.

In fact, it was relatively close at hand because the Germans had naval bases around the coast of occupied Norway as well as airfields. The purpose of the convoy making a wide sweep to the north towards Spitzbergen was to keep well away from the Norwegian coastline to avoid attacks from the Luftwaffe, German submarines and surface vessels. The *Llanstephan Castle* formed part of one of the earliest convoys carrying aid for Russia and only nine east-bound Russian convoys, comprising 63 ships in all were to sail before the end of the year.

The boys on the liner were lucky not to have encountered trouble during the voyage but these were early days in the terrible and costly battle which future Russian convoys would have to fight. There were certainly U-boats about because while they were sailing in far northern waters in late August Coastal Command captured U-boat *570* south of Iceland. Lockheed Hudsons of 269 Squadron dropped depth charges, forced the damaged U-boat to surface and kept circling until a tug escorted by a destroyer took the boat in tow.

Blissfully unaware that the *Llanstephan Castle* could have been attacked at any minute the RAF personnel carried on with their cruise-like existence. This sense of unreality and most un-troopship like atmosphere was enhanced by the fact that the vessel's stylish accommodation also carried a number of civilian passengers. Notables included Vernon Bartlett MP; Wallace Carrol, an American journalist; Mrs Charlotte Haldane; the Polish artist Topolsky and members of a Polish Legation and a Czechoslovakian mission heading for Moscow. The dignitaries obliged by giving a series of lectures on their particular subjects to liven up the journey. These proved so popular that lecturers gave a repeat performance in the afternoon because the main dining room could only accommodate about 250.

The Wing was naturally keen to hear anything of interest concerning Russia and was fed large doses of 'gen' ranging from Mrs Haldane's 'Domestic Life in Russia', to Flight Lieutenant Hodson's three lectures on his experiences in that country. Hodson had been born there and lived much of his life in the Russia of the Tsars. Apart from Hubert Griffith's lecture on Soviet Russia from a historical standpoint interpreters gave the boys a crash course in the language ensuring that most knew a few basic words before they docked.

This period gave the Wing a chance of settling down as a rather large family type of unit in that they were all literally 'in the same boat together'. As is usual in these circumstances when men congregate with time on their hands certain characters and personalities make their impact and bind the thing together. One of these was Flight Sergeant Barkus who was in charge of Wing discipline. When he first had the Wing on parade Barkus stalked up and down eyeing everybody, and, having let that sink in, he roared out, 'You know who I am? My name is Barkus. Get it, Barkus. That's who I am. And I'm known as Barkus the bastard.' Thumping his chest he carried on, 'I'll repeat that for those of you that have cloth ears. Barkus the bastard, and I'll tell you lot I did not get that name for nothing. I've got my eye on you, all of you, every single one so you just watch it, see!'

After a journey of a little over two weeks the liner turned south and began groping its way down through the White Sea steaming towards the port of Archangel. It was an electrifying moment when they caught their first glimpse of the Russian coastline and realized for the first time that their incredible adventure was about to 'kick off' and the holiday aboard ship was almost over.

It was a long journey of about four or five hours up river to where the ship finally docked and everybody crowded the ship's rails watching the local scenery and taking interest in local activities. 'I don't think any of us had ever seen so much wood in various stages of production', Micky Turner said, 'Each side of the river was solid with logs interspersed with the odd hut or mill.'

Ginger Carter remembered hearing rifle shots before he and other pilots were cleared away from the ship's rails. Apparently their uniforms were similar to German ones and local Russians, thinking that they were prisoners of war, started firing at the ship. The only casualty was a member of the crew who was hit in the arm but as Ginger Carter said, 'It did make us realize right away that the locals were a pretty wild bunch and we would have to watch it. Also it was only a matter of weeks since we had been enemies.'

As they got closer into the dock they were surprised to see women working as navvies on the loading and unloading of ships and it looked as if the workforce in the docks area was predominantly female. When the ship dropped anchor she was about fifty feet from the side of the river because of the depth of the water and immediately hundreds of Russians began building a wooden dock structure towards the side of the ship. They were told on board that this operation was going to take three or four days before the ship could be unloaded and it would be a race against time to get the ship back to sea before the river became frozen over.

Looking down from the ship at the frenzied scene of activity going on around them the airmen were naturally keen to use their land legs and get a first-hand impression of what this part of Russia was really like. They were itching to get going and couldn't understand why they were kept hanging about. In order to get some exercise they were eventually allowed to march around the area in groups but at no time were airmen to be without rifles or officers and NCOs without their revolvers.

During the voyage Wing Commander Ramsbottom Isherwood had been busy working out a plan of action if the group from Moscow, who were to advise and assist him hadn't arrived. He intended to shift the bulk of the Main Party by road to Murmansk in its own transport. This operation, he thought, could be accomplished in relays but to his horror he found out shortly after docking that there didn't happen to be any roads around the coastline of the White Sea leading north towards the port of Murmansk.

This was a considerable blow because he had transport ready to roll off the ship and time was an important factor. It would have made life so much easier if the convoy had been able to dock at Murmansk in the first place but the Russians had advised against it. Murmansk, they said, was only a few miles from the front line and well within range of German bombers which regularly attacked the port and the town itself. He knew that it would take some considerable time to unload the convoy and he assumed that the Russians knew what they were doing, but docking at Archangel did make life difficult.

Much to his relief, after docking he learned that the Moscow contingent had arrived and a conference had been arranged on board a Russian Admiralty yacht moored alongside one of the many wooden jetties in the port. His major problem was that he needed to co-ordinate the Wing's routing programme as soon as possible. The advance party led by Flight Lieutenants Rook and Cottam, for example, had gone on a previous ship with essential equipment and stores and he was anxious to find out where they were and how they were getting on.

The two squadrons in the aircraft carrier, *Argus,* were still at sea and were scheduled to fly off the carrier into Vianga. Somehow he would have to transport ground staff and personnel to Vianga to get everything organized on the airfield ready to receive the squadrons when they flew in. They were due in a little over a week and Vianga was some 300 miles away.

There was also the question of the crated Hurricanes carried in the convoy. There were 200 of these and he needed fifteen of them to be uncrated and assembled as soon as possible. Those Hurricanes, when ready, were to be flown into Vianga airfield by the pilots who had travelled on the liner and would make up the Squadron's complement.

Like all good commanding officers, Isherwood remained aloof and therefore able to take a detached view of any situation without being personally or emotionally involved. He had a good and experienced team of officers and NCOs, but the overall responsibility for the Expedition was his alone. The situation in which he found himself when the *Llanstephan Castle* docked at Archangel demanded a cool head and plenty of nerve. His men were about to disembark into an area remote and desolate where communications were practically non-existent. There was no common language and he was virtually in the hands of a people who had only been allies for a matter of weeks. The Germans had advanced to within a few miles of his destination, Murmansk, and from information that he had gathered the war in Russia had reached a critical stage.

Most men would have been daunted by the problems facing Isherwood as, in company with his wireless and engineering officers and his Wing Adjutant, he was conducted to the Russian Admiralty yacht. But the Wing Commander was a phlegmatic character and a senior regular RAF officer who, quite apart from his ability to command, knew more about flying than his younger contemporaries, having been a test pilot for several years.

When they caught sight of the Russian yacht the party of RAF officers was surprised to see an extremely smart, white-painted modern motor vessel about the size of a British Naval sloop. The Admiral's cabin was gleaming with polished brass and satin wood and Isherwood was somewhat relieved to meet Air Vice-Marshal Collier who had travelled from Moscow as the Russian-speaking head of the British Air Mission. Collier was in company with a young looking Russian Rear-Admiral and two British Naval liaison officers and Isherwood got the feeling that now they would be able to get things moving because it was imperative that wireless personnel and equipment should be transported to Murmansk as soon as possible.

When they got down to business Isherwood was told that the plan formulated in Moscow was for the Wing to be transported in a series of special trains which had already been requisitioned. This sounded sense to Isherwood but then came the bad news. A report had come through on the day that the *Llanstephan Castle* was making her way into the port of Archangel that the Luftwaffe had bombed the Kandalaksha-Murmansk railway line and put it out of action.

There was only one thing that the conference could do and that was to utilize all air and sea resources and make use of the railway when it was repaired. It was decided to send a small party of wireless technicians in two aircraft from the Keg-Ostrov airfield outside Archangel — one aircraft on the next day and the other on the day following. A party of 200 under the Wing Commander was to be transported by two British destroyers, HMS *Electra* and HMS *Active* and would leave within 48 hours. Two days later another group was to go by Russian tramp steamer to Kandalaksha and from there by train to the airfield at Vianga. Finally, two more parties were to do the entire journey by train once the rail link had been repaired.

It was a complex plan but the best that anybody could have hatched out in the circumstances and Isherwood was fairly certain that most of them would have a 'hairy' time before they eventually arrived at Vianga. For the time being, however, the liner was serving as a splendid hotel and 'set them up' for the rigours of their travels across the tundra.

There had been no contact with the Russian civilian population until one RAF officer, who was watching work in progress on the quayside, decided to lend a hand. He recorded the experience in his diary:

'Standing on the deck of the transport one afternoon, while waiting to get orders to move up, the last day that the troopship was in port, I saw a couple of old Russian lumber-men and a party of a dozen Russian girls sawing up and loading timber into lorries as they arrived at the dockside. After they had loaded up all the timber that was in sight, they moved off to the next railway shed, and from the coming and going of lorries it was obvious that the sawing and loading up was still going forward. I thought after three weeks almost stationary existence on board ship, that I'd go ashore and get some exercise by helping.

'The party was under the command of a girl of about twenty, a qualified engineer. They worked away for three hours like absolute fury, the engineer-girl working the hardest of the lot. No one was looking on or supervising — but the speed of the work was prodigious. Once a lorry was loaded up with sawn timber, the girls would sit down for a breather and start smoking and singing. And then, when another lorry would come up, they'd start in all over again.

'About half-way through the loading and sawing I felt that I had strained every muscle of my body, and my hands were raw with working a two-handed saw — but every time I sat down for a rest, there would appear another girl at the end of a log weighing half-a-ton and waiting to be helped carry it, or another girl waiting for someone to help her saw it in half — and back one would have to go to the treadmill of labour out of pure shame — explaining that one had been three weeks aboard ship, and one was not quite in one's natural athletic condition...

'The whole thing was, on their part, a marvellous exhibition of enthusiasm, energy and concentration. When they had finished loading every piece of timber in sight, they got to and swept down the whole quay-side (including all the rubbish chucked off the transport), a task which took an hour, and then buzzed off home.'

* * *

While Wing Commander Ramsbottom Isherwood had been in conference on the Russian Admiralty yacht the aircraft carrier HMS *Argus* was ploughing its way towards Murmansk. There was no luxury cruise atmosphere on board this vessel as Wag Haw and his chum Ibby Waud found out shortly after they had embarked from Gourock on the outskirts of Glasgow.

Their problems began when the carrier anchored off Scapa Flow awaiting instructions to proceed on its Arctic voyage. The Squadron pilots had expected that the ship would just call in and then sail for Murmansk but after a few days lying at anchor there were rumours that if the boat didn't get clearance to go in the immediate future then the operation might be aborted.

Wag was getting rather 'brassed off' with life because there was no excitement and nothing to do except to go ashore with the matelots in their jollyboats during the afternoons for a piss-up and sometimes visit battleships in the vicinity. It might have been more fun if they had actually had a pub in which to meet the locals and relax. But there was nothing to do but sit in a ghastly long wooden hut which served as a NAAFI providing booze but little atmosphere.

Life on board was a little cramped because the *Argus* was a converted merchant ship which had been captured from the Italians during World War One and it was not designed for the job it was doing. Most of the superstructure had been cut away to allow for a flight deck which was about 360 ft long. Wag and Ibby, together with other NCO pilots, messed with the Petty Officers and had to 'lash and stow' hammocks, which at first was a joke but soon became a routine.

Just when they thought that the whole show was about to be called off and much to their relief, they heard the tannoy crackling out and the voice of the ship's Captain announcing that they were about to set sail. They could feel the old boat vibrating from stem to stern as she slowly made her way out of Scapa Flow in a flat calm and mucky weather but for them it was a great sensation knowing that they were really on the move at last.

It took a little while for them to appreciate that they had finally cut adrift from the old country and were actually on their way to Russia. Being on board a Naval carrier was a new experience but as the excitement of being at sea on a wartime footing began to wear off the trip became rather a boring affair. The food was good but there was little to do except to play cards, attend the odd talk and walk round the decks being careful not to get in the way of the Navy.

For most of the time the old *Argus* sailed through a blanket of mist and all they could see was the marker trailed by the ship in front bobbing up and down. The daily rum ration always went down well but other than that there was no booze for the NCO pilots: the officers, of course, had their wardroom bar. Wag and Ibby often went below decks to have a look at their new Hurricanes which they had never flown before. They weren't complete because the wings had not been bolted on but it was fun to sit in the cockpit, feel the controls and talk about the jazzed-up Merlin engine in their Mark IIs and having the destructive power of twelve Browning machine-guns at the touch of a button.

Both men were mad keen to get to Russia and 'have a go'. As Wag kept on saying, 'It's all happening out there, Ibby. That's where the action is, chum.' This may have sounded like bravado or a line-shoot to the uninitiated but there wasn't a trace of that in either of them. Wag still needed to convince himself that he was as good as anybody and better than most in aerial combat. All he wanted was the challenge and he genuinely felt that he would get plenty of that in Russia. For Ibby, Russia was going to be his chance to build up his combat experience.

Walking around the flight deck of the carrier made them aware of what a short distance they had to get their Hurricanes off. There were two Grumman Martlets on the flight deck ready to take off in defence of the carrier and these naturally attracted the interest of the Hurricane pilots. They were short, tubby aircraft equipped with four .5 machine-guns and looked rather like miniature versions of the later P-47 Thunderbolt. The Naval chaps who flew them said that they had a useful turn of speed and were extremely manoeuvrable. Fortunately, as far as the Hurricane pilots were concerned, the Martlets had remained stationary on the flight deck without having to scramble in the carrier's defence.

There was no sign of the weather lifting as the *Argus* steamed further north and finally turned south in the direction of the Russian coast. When she initially stood off the coast there was insufficient wind to get the Hurricanes off and this calm lasted for some considerable time as she steamed slowly in circles waiting for a blow. Eventually word got around that the *Argus* was running very short of fuel and if the Navy couldn't get the Hurricanes off early before breakfast on the following morning then the entire project might have to be abandoned.

Night was practically non-existent because the sun only went down for about half-an-hour at midnight. Not that they had seen much of it during the voyage, having ploughed their way through mist for most of the time. Assembling and getting 24 Hurricanes airborne for Russia was going to be a fairly complex operation. The Martlets would have to be dismantled and stowed below before the Hurricanes could be brought up in dribs and drabs by lift and assembled alongside the flight deck. There was only room for six Hurricanes up top and they would have to take off to make room for more aircraft coming up from below deck. Meanwhile, the *Argus* would be steaming into wind at her maximum speed of about 17 knots and it was vital that the assembly operations were carried out efficiently and quickly.

Prangs on the flight deck were always a possibility and none of the Hurricane pilots had ever taken off from a carrier before so it was going to be a fairly 'hairy' operation for all concerned. The Naval pilots had given the boys some 'gen' about taking off explaining that they should give the ramp at the end of the flight deck a fair thump and this would help to get the machine airborne. Also, they mentioned that compasses this far north tended to rotate and it was difficult to get any kind of accurate reading. Therefore, it was arranged that the escorting destroyer would lay off the carrier and point in the direction of the Russian coast. All they had to do then was to hit the coast and turn right until they saw Vianga airfield on their left a few miles inland!

The two Squadron commanders, Tony Rook of 81 and Tony Miller of 134 briefed their chaps, telling them not to hang around and as soon as a vic formation was airborne to do a circuit of the carrier, pick up the destroyer, fly down the length of it and then make for the Russian coast. Finally, they were warned to keep a sharp look out for bandits in the vicinity. All being well 134 Squadron was to be first off on the following morning, 7 September. They had been aboard *Argus* for twenty days, having spent ten of them at Scapa Flow waiting to sail, and everybody was 'raring to go'.

It was a grey, chill morning when Wag Haw had a mug of cocoa and started to make his way up to the flight deck. He was wearing battledress, flying boots and Mae West and carrying a small bag containing his toilet gear. The previous evening he had gone down to the hangar below and left his helmet, goggles and oxygen mask in the cockpit of his aircraft 'H for Harry' telling the lads to treat her gently when she came up in the lift.

He found a convenient spot to watch the proceedings in a gangway off the flight deck and reckoned that he would be about number seventeen out of the 24 pilots taking off. The sea was calm and he could feel the breeze on his cheeks as the first Hurricanes appeared from the lift. Although it was very early autumn in Northern Russia and a grey, overcast day he didn't feel cold at all and stood there waiting for the action to commence knowing that he was going to take part in it within the next half-an-hour or so.

He could feel the boat shuddering and vibrating when the crews began running up the Rolls-Royce Merlin engines of the Hurricanes. It seemed as if the old aircraft carrier *Argus* had sensed the occasion and was picking up her skirts and having a go herself before the fighters took off. She would have to go all out in this light wind, he thought, to give the boys a chance — they would need all her seventeen knots plus the wind speed to lift off from the short length of deck.

He stared at Tony Miller's Hurricane revving up against the brakes as the batman gave him the signal and the Hurricane roared down the deck approaching the wooden sloping ramp at the end. Tony did exactly what the Naval pilots had suggested and thumped straight up the ramp pulling his stick back to get airborne. Fascinated, Wag saw the Hurricane waddle into the air like a well-fed duck and could see that the undercarriage had been damaged by the ramp and wouldn't retract.

Other pilots had watched the proceedings and realized that somehow they would have to yank their Hurricanes off the deck before the ramp. Not that the Naval chaps had given them 'duff gen', it was simply that the Hurricane wasn't stressed underneath like the Naval Martlets and its undercarriage couldn't take the crunch. In Wag's opinion the Martlet flew like a constipated turkey and he was going to make damn sure that he got his Hurricane off without having to belly land in Russia.

As soon as he caught sight of 'H for Harry' popping up from the depths of the carrier he walked over to take a close look at the proceedings. The boys worked incredibly quickly and within minutes he had climbed into the cockpit with the engine running awaiting his turn to be guided and manipulated on to the flight deck. It felt good to be back in the seat once again. He hadn't flown for well over a month and the smell of his aeroplane and the feel of the controls in his hands and at his feet was like a drug urging him to open her up and break free.

He saw his number one roar down the deck as they manoeuvred 'H' into position and he remembered the ground crew telling him that he was not fully armed and that only six of his twelve machine-guns had been fitted in order to reduce weight. Putting down partial flap, he gently opened the throttle holding the machine against the brakes while keeping an eye on the batman. The Merlin sounded sweet and eager and on the signal he shoved open the throttle and let her go. The wooden ramp standing about two or three feet high loomed up to meet him like an express train as he yanked back on the stick and to his great relief she became unstuck and floated into the air. With the throttle wide open he eased the stick forward to pick up flying speed and she dived down towards the sea before gently easing up into a climbing turn.

Retracting flaps and adjusting controls he looked around and spotted his number one circling the carrier. It was a great moment to be back in business again as he tucked in behind his leader. Down below the old *Argus* looked like an elongated tin can, having no superstructure and with steam coming out of its backside. There was no bridge and he wondered how the Naval chaps had managed to steer the bloody thing, but that wasn't his worry any longer because he was free of it and in a world of his own.

They levelled off at 1,300 ft as the last Hurricane caught up with them and made the vic formation. To his right he could see the destroyer pointing in the direction of the Russian coast and as they flew down the length of it he set his gyro on zero as a directional aid. It made him giggle thinking about it because Russia was such a bloody great country that they couldn't possibly miss it!

Twenty minutes later he caught his first glimpse of the grey undulating coastline washed by the Barents Sea. It seemed to reflect the grey drabness of the blanket of cloud which covered the horizon and there was no sign of habitation. He pumped the throttle to keep station as the vic formation turned starboard and started flying along the coastline in search of Vianga airfield. Down below was a wilderness of scrub, rivulets and lakes and he shuddered to think what would happen if his Merlin suddenly packed up and he had to come down in that god-forsaken territory.

Despite the grey cloud, visibility was good and they were able to

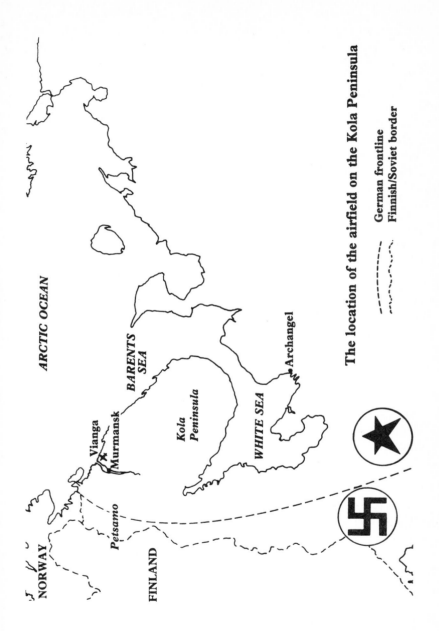

ARCTIC OCEAN

BARENTS SEA

Vianga
Murmansk

Petsamo

NORWAY

FINLAND

Kola Peninsula

WHITE SEA

Archangel

The location of the airfield on the Kola Peninsula

German frontline
Finnish/Soviet border

spot the Hurricanes on Vianga airfield without any trouble. It was a large base, oval shaped and about three miles in length from east to west, which Wag thought was obviously the direction of the prevailing winds in those parts. From the air the place seemed to be in some sort of bowl surrounded by hillocks and wooded areas. There were no runways and the surface was covered in a grey, sandy coloured substance presenting a dull and drab looking picture.

In the circuit Wag was surprised at not seeing any of the normal buildings and hangers which characterize bases at home and thought that they must be bloody well camouflaged or non-existent. Throttling back and putting down flap on the approach he had a laugh when he saw a Hurricane on its belly with a group of men standing around it and thought to himself what an impression the Wing must have created with the Russkies when the first Hurricane to fly in did a smart belly landing!

His Hurricane bucketed about a bit as he landed due to the rough and uneven surface, the primitive nature of which surprised him in the circumstances as he had been told that Vianga was a major operational base. Anyway, at long last he was actually on Russian soil and as the chums from the advance party waved him into dispersals he felt keyed up and ready to go.

Ibby Waud recalled his turn to take off from the carrier *Argus*. 'It all seemed to happen so quickly,' he said, 'Strap in, helmet on, do the old familiar cockpit check, plus on this occasion putting some degrees of flap down. Left hand on throttle with the engine running sweetly and responding to the touch. RT crackling in my ears and a great feeling that after a lay off from flying I was back in business and in charge again. My turn comes for take off. Chocks away! GO! Smoothly but immediately I open up the throttle to maximum revs and then release the hand brake. I tell myself to keep the bloody nose up — for Chrissake!

'A momentary view of the sides of the flight deck lasting only seconds and the *Argus* disappears. That was my last glimpse of her. Then I am suspended over the waves feeling like a goose flapping to take off and gain flying speed. Wheels up and I soon sense the wings properly biting into the air and up I go. At twelve o'clock above I spot a little group of Hurricanes doing a wide left hand circuit nicely placed for me so I climb and join them. Somewhere far below is the *Argus* and a destroyer positioned to point in the direction of Murmansk but I was busy keeping station in formation and didn't see them.

'We press on bravely in formation, but for ages, or it seems like ages, we are suspended in an unreal world of greyness. I wonder where the hell we are and hope that the CO, old Tony Rook, picked the right destroyer to take his direction from. Morbid thoughts go through my mind like it's either going to be Russia or a watery grave. We fly through more whispery grey cloud but it seems thinner and the sky looks lighter. Then — oh, joy! — we are out of the clag and quite clearly, there ahead, is the coastline and the clouds have lifted. I wish that Winston Churchill or whoever had this crazy idea could see us now as we are sweeping grandly over the Russian coast.

Flying fairly low — I suppose about 2,000 ft — we follow the course of the river. I look down with intense curiosity. The only sign of life is the odd log cabin along the banks of the river; the rest is a rocky desolation stretching as far as the eye can see. Ahead is the open space of Vianga aerodrome. Soon we are on the circuit flying over a village which looks like a cowboy town. But there is no time for sightseeing. No runway, of course; the aerodrome is hard sand. We land in good order, switch off and jump down from our aircraft. The long and improbable journey which began at Leconfield has been successfully completed and we are standing firmly on Russian soil.'

Chapter 6
Floating hotel

While the Russian labour force was busy man-handling and
building the wooden dock structure to fill in the gap between the
quay and the *Llanstephan Castle* the RAF contingent remaining on
board was still enjoying the excellent cuisine and hotel-style
accommodation.

The first men to leave were those needed immediately at Vianga
and they were taken off the liner by river craft and transported to
the airfield at Keg-Ostrov on the other side of the river opposite
Archangel. These consisted mainly of communications technicians
whose job it was to set up an RT station at Vianga for the incoming
Hurricanes from the aircraft carrier *Argus*. From Keg Ostrov they
were flown in two aircraft on successive days to Vianga which was
some 300 miles away. The first aircraft made a successful trip but
the second, a large undefended Douglas, ran into enemy aircraft
and was forced to do a smart about turn and head back to base. The
party was fortunate because the Luftwaffe aircraft operating from
bases in Norway were at the very limit of their range and couldn't
chase the Douglas and shoot it down. However, the party
concerned made the trip on the following day without incident.

Shortly afterwards another party of 200 were put aboard the
destroyers *Electra* and *Active* and made the trip around the coast of
Murmansk in 22 hours. Flight Sergeant Micky Turner was on
board HMS *Active* and found it the most interesting trip so far
despite the luxury of the liner. The sailors were a terrific bunch
and most hospitable. 'They showed us', he said, 'most of the

workings of the old destroyer, whose back-end seemed to shake uncontrollably: the ship was obviously in need of a refit.' They had a few reservists on board who told him that they had joined *Electra* in September 1939 and still hadn't been back home. The weather was very thick indeed and *Electra* had to feel her way back through the White Sea to the Kola inlet where they were to be met by a Russian destroyer which would guide them through the minefields. The Russian boat failed to materialize but with the aid of Asdic they got through to Murmansk.

While 151 Wing had been at sea Prime Minister Winston Churchill had telegraphed Premier Stalin on 28 August telling him that he had been searching in every possible way to give help to Russia in her splendid resistance, pending the long term arrangements under discussion with the United States, and he went on to say that forty Hurricanes should reach Murmansk by the end of the first week in September with a further 200 for the use of Russian pilots.

Churchill was, of course, referring to 151 Wing which was becoming a useful card in his hand at this particular time when it was vital that he should be seen by the Russians to be doing something positive. Despite the enormity of the conflict going on in Russia the arrival of the RAF Expedition had created an impact in the corridors of Moscow. A delegation of high-ranking Soviet officers was to meet the Hurricanes when the squadrons flew into Vianga and the Russians in Archangel and Murmansk, although in desperate circumstances had gone to no end of trouble to do everything they could to help right from the very beginning.

The Wing's engineer-officer, Flight Lieutenant Gittins, Warrant Officer Hards and their labour force of rank-and-file technical airmen on board the liner were soon to discover what life in Northern Russia was like and how the Russians would help them out. These chaps were to be left behind at Archangel to uncrate and assemble fifteen Hurricanes ready to fly out to Vianga.

Gittins, who led the party, was a regular officer and older than his compatriots. A cheerful and bubbly man with a keen sense of humour he was of average height, slimly built and had a rather thin, drawn face. His gang became known in RAF terms as the 'Erection Party' the different connotations of which caused much ribald comment.

The party consisting of two officers, one Warrant Officer, three Flight Sergeants, two Sergeants and thirty airmen, disembarked from the *Llanstephan Castle* shortly after 9.00 am and went upstream in a river steamer heading for a place called Keg Island. Their destination was Keg-Ostrov aerodrome which was about one hour away and they arrived to find the crated Hurricanes, weighing three-and-a-half tons each, dumped outside the hangars on a rough and uneven mud flat.

A crowd of interested bystanders gathered around watching them taking wireless equipment for the WT ground-station into one of the hangars. The Russians stood there talking excitedly among themselves and gesticulating as if they were watching some kind of variety performance but with the language barrier the airmen had to relay on 'dumb crambo' techniques to make contact.

When they started to unpack one aircraft to use the packing case for housing the WT station they quickly discovered that many essential assembly tools including airscrew spanners were missing. Although the 500 or more personnel of all ranks had been assembled and despatched for the Expedition, someone else somewhere had put together what they thought would be needed to assemble, run and maintain the Hurricanes. The result was that special tools were not found and tropical covers were included to insulate Merlin engines in the Arctic Circle!

Engineers the world over have a common understanding over such practical matters and Flight Lieutenant Gittins quickly established a rapport with the Russian engineer officer who improvised by rule of thumb methods and made the necessary tools in his workshops. It wasn't long before the Russian workshops produced insulated covers too, complete with a trunk attached to the underside. Then they provided a 'hot air' lorry which gave a hot air boost through the trunk to keep the Rolls-Royce engines warm and comfortable.

Gittins, like Hubert Griffith the Wing Adjutant, kept a diary of events and recorded that on the first day on Keg-Ostrov aerodrome the midday meal consisted of cabbage soup, beef steak and rice followed by stewed fruit. At 1.30 pm, he said, work was resumed with one group taking a second Hurricane from its crate while the wireless chaps erected the WT station. The Russians provided petrol and oil supplies and by 2.30 pm accumulators were being charged. An hour later the second aircraft, complete with components, was being pushed up to the hangar.

Tea, Russian style, was at 4.30 pm, in a glass without milk with dark brown bread and very pale butter. By 6.30 pm the third Hurricane was being pushed into a hangar and shortly afterwards the WT station had been completed. Owing to a lack of lifting tackle they packed up work at 7.00 pm and had a supper of fried fresh pike, minced meat cutlets and cocoa, having managed six-and-a-half working hours during the day.

The 'Erection Party' was astonished and amused to be billeted in an ancient river paddle-steamer looking like the *Mississippi Belle*. In true naval fashion the troops occupied the lower deck, and the officers' cabins plus dining saloon and kitchen were up above. Her popular nickname became 'the Winkle Barge' but some called her 'the Missouri Scow.' On the first night aboard Gittins was awakened by two airmen who were covered in bumps and blood saying that they had been eaten alive by bugs. Gittins told them to keep their cabin lights on and hope for the best! That was all he could do in the circumstances because he had no medical supplies but he made a mental note to ask the Russians on the following morning if they could disinfect the vessel.

Gittins' main problem at that time was the safety factor of the lifting tackle which he considered was not large enough to take the risk. The Russians obliged on the next day by loaning him three 1,000 kilo cranes, some cable and bolts. By constructing a three-point suspension from each of the upper front wing attachment bolts and the front engine slinging rig he managed to lift the aircraft until it was standing on its undercarriage. The winding up process on all three cranes together was hard work because it had to be done by hand.

The assembly operation was causing quite a local stir and Russians would come up and stroke the wings. They were naturally curious because they hadn't seen RAF personnel in action before and had never seen a Hurricane. During the morning high-ranking local Army and Navy Air Arm officers visited the hangar to watch the proceedings. Gittins and his party were beginning to feel like VIPs with all the attention and co-operation.

A lunch of potato soup, steak, roast potatoes and stewed fruit got everybody in shape for the afternoon shift during which two more aircraft were pushed under the cranes and hoisted up until they stood on their undercarriages. Tail units were fitted and armourers got busy on the machine-guns. Russian tea was taken at 4.30 pm and by 7.00 pm two Hurricanes had wings loosely bolted into position.

It started raining that evening and apart from the weather Gittins decided not to start unpacking further aircraft because he lacked the facilities to erect them. He split his working party into three gangs and carried on fitting tail units and main-planes. A supper of ham and cucumber was taken at 7.00 pm and afterwards work continued on the wings of a third aircraft.

He had asked the Russians for some temporary accommodation for his men so that 'the Winkle Barge' could be disinfected and they found a house which proved to be very clean and comfortable but about four miles from the airfield. Much to his surprise and delight the local authorities loaned him a car and two lorries which turned up at 11.00 pm. They all piled into the transport after working for almost thirteen hours.

By 7.00 am on the third day the airmen had arrived from their temporary quarters and were tucking into a breakfast of smoked salmon, warm breakfast sausage and potatoes. Good progress was made on the three aircraft until lunch at 12.15 — the meat rissoles now being referred to as 'Archangel-rissoles' by the wags! During the afternoon a fourth and fifth aircraft were unpacked from crates and pushed into the hangar. The usual Russian tea was taken at 4.30 pm.

Gittins made a special mention in his diary of a dish they had for supper that evening. It was called *'Byelooga'* and consisted of minced meat wrapped in white cabbage leaves — a rather dramatic change from a UK fare of egg, sausage, corned beef and chips! The Russian food from the outset had been very good indeed, but rather rich compared with the wartime diet at home. Consequently some of the airmen started to develop tummy troubles and were treated by a medical officer who came up from the *Llanstephan Castle*.

The main party scheduled to go to Murmansk by train still hadn't left the liner, either because there were no trains available or because the railway line bombed by the Germans was under repair. Life was becoming rather dull and boring so day trips into Archangel were arranged. A few pounds worth of roubles were handed out but anybody going had to be armed and they were warned to stay in groups. They were picked off the liner in rather strange looking boats rather like coal barges with glass tops, but after several day excursions the trips were considered too dangerous and were called off.

Most of the Archangel Russians were of the Mongolian type who were very tough and wild. They were men who would cut anybody's throat and throw them in the river for a few roubles or a watch. Dressed in quilted jackets, fur hats and big fur boots they looked and indeed were a murderous bunch. By contrast there were other Russians, usually officers, who were more European in features and very pleasant. One could hardly blame the Russians for being trigger happy at this stage of the war and the sight of RAF personnel in uniform and walking about Archangel was asking for the kind of trouble that they had experienced on the boat when local Russians thought they were German prisoners and took pot shots at them.

The pilots on board were taken up river to see how their beloved Hurricanes were progressing on Keg-Ostrov aerodrome which made a break and at least brought them in contact with aeroplanes once again. By that time Flight Lieutenant Gittins was on his fifth day and everything was going well except for the 'grumbleguts'. He told Sergeant Pilot Ginger Carter and his chum John Mulroy that two Corporals had gone down with it that morning.

Ginger Carter, who was particularly good at maths, was fascinated by Gittins' account about the lost spanners which were very special and vital. They urgently needed them for fitting airscrews and sparking plugs. The day before Gittins had contacted the local Russian engineer-officer and asked him if he could somehow produce two spanners, giving him a sketch of what he wanted and an airscrew as a sample. Work was being carried out on five aircraft that day in preparation for ground-testing. By four o'clock in the afternoon the Russian engineer chum, grinning all over his face, arrived with the spanners and five airscrews and the inlet sparking-plugs were duly fitted.

That day proved to be a rather special one in the history of the 'Erection Party' at Keg-Ostrov. Gittins told Ginger Carter: 'After tea, I contacted the authorities and asked for some petrol and they promised it for 6.00 pm. The petrol ('Benzine') arrived to time, with a chamois-leather funnel and a comic pump to extract it from the barrels. We managed to find out how the pump worked, and to fill the first aircraft.

'Excitement was now really great among our Russian friends who were keen to see the first Hurricane engine actually running. At 8.35 pm we turned the engine over by starter-battery until the oil gauge showed a movement. (We had to use this method as there were no facilities for making a priming-pump.) At 8.37 pm the main switches were put on and the engine sprang to life, all instruments reading correctly. There were plenty of cheers and clapping on the part of spectators.'

Several Russian Generals and Colonels came to see the Hurricanes being assembled. The officers' dining room on board 'the Winkle Barge' became a focal point for lunches and dinners, during which a special kind of relationship was established with the Russians and especially those commanding the battles on the Northern Russian front. For example, on the evening when the first Hurricane Merlin engine coughed, spluttered and roared into life a large supper party was held to celebrate the event. Russian officials included General Grigorieff, Colonel Eelegin (Naval Air Service), and Major Kuznetsov, Commandant of the Keg-Ostrov Aerodrome. Air-Vice-Marshal Collier, the Russian-speaking head of the British Air Mission in Moscow, and Group Captain Bird headed up the RAF contingent.

At last, on the sixth day, three of the Hurricanes which had been assembled and serviced were pushed out of the hangar for air testing. Flight Lieutenant Mickey Rook and Pilot Officers Artie Holmes and Woolaston from 81 Squadron arrived from the liner to put the aircraft through their paces. Before getting airborne, however, the three officers were to have their first experience of lunch — Russian style!

After the cuisine on the liner the pilots had mixed feelings when confronted by *Gooloopsi*, potato soup, and stewed *Oornik* particularly as they were about to perform gyrations in the air to demonstrate the manoeuvrability of their Hawker Hurricanes. Local anti-aircraft batteries and troops were alerted that British fighters would be flying in the vicinity well before Mickey Rook and the boys climbed into their machines. It was a grey, overcast afternoon with a cloud base of only about 1,000 ft so they didn't have much space for fun and games.

Russian tea was another experience for them and during that time a message came through that the People's Commissar of the Fleet, an Admiral, in company with the Admiral of the Archangel Naval Force and his Chief-of-Staff had arrived on the aerodrome and would like to see the Hurricanes perform. Any pilot testing his machine in front of 'top brass' automatically becomes a salesman for his machine and the boys were well aware that they were 'on parade'. Tight turns and low level beat-ups were really the only manoeuvres which could be performed in the weather conditions prevailing at the time but they put on a good show and the Russian Admirals were obviously impressed by what they had seen.

At the end of Gittins' first week at Keg-Ostrov, oil and petrol engineers from Moscow suddenly appeared on the scene and began asking innumerable questions regarding oils and fuels. Britain had been using a higher octane aviation fuel in the northern European theatre and the Russians wanted to know all about this development especially as its application improved aircraft performance considerably.

That evening the airmen were given English food for a change: the bully beef, tinned potatoes and pickles went down rather well, especially with a free issue of beer. They had been working for about twelve hours a day and bearing in mind that their billet was four miles away this wasn't bad going! Low cloud and rain had turned the rough, muddy airfield into a quagmire and they had been operating under extremely difficult conditions with a few hand-wound cranes and spanners improvised by the Russians.

More Russian Generals and Admirals came to see the show as pilots arrived from the *Llanstephan Castle* to test their aircraft. Finally, within a matter of nine days fifteen Hurricanes had been uncrated, jacked up, lowered on to their undercarriages, had their wings and tail planes fitted and had been armed, fuelled and tested ready for the flight to Vianga.

Apart from doing a good job of work in difficult conditions the 'Erection Party' had continually been on parade in a technical working sense in front of high Russian officials. Gittins and his men were ambassadors for the RAF in every sense of the word. The Hurricane was a novelty for the Russians, as was the opportunity to watch the RAF at work and to put it mildly they were fascinated by everything that was going on at the Keg-Ostrov aerodrome.

The pilots had been confined on the liner for some time and were naturally bubbling over to climb into their machines and 'let go'. Russian troops and civilians alike in the Archangel area soon got the message that the British fighters meant business loud and clear as Hurricanes screamed low overhead. On the day that the fifteen Hurricanes took off for Murmansk the Russian officers gave the pilots a farewell party.

Ginger Carter remembered that they were given large glasses of vodka and jars of caviar and stood around eating it with spoons like jam. It tasted a bit oily, he said, but we were told that it was very good for the 'working parts' so we stuffed it down. Flight Lieutenant Mickey Rook who was going to lead the formation kept a watchful eye on his young pilots and warned them to be careful if they weren't used to strong drink. 'Those Russians will have a big laugh', he said with a grin, 'if any of you chaps prang on take-off'.

Chapter 7
Vianga — Murmansk

When Wag Haw jumped off the mainplane of his Hurricane he found it almost impossible to believe that he was actually in Russia and the Squadron had at last 'made it'. Other Hurricanes were still taxiing into dispersal and swinging round before the pilots revved up and cut engines. Checking his watch he was surprised to find that he had been airborne for an hour and ten minutes since he had staggered off the deck of the old carrier. After his somewhat 'hairy' take-off the flight had been uneventful, which had surprised him. He couldn't understand why the Luftwaffe hadn't come after them right away and had a go. Opening a capacious compartment in the side of the Hurricane he pulled out his parachute bag filled with clothing and personal items and walked over to dispersal.

Ground crews were pushing a Hurricane backwards and trying to get it into a semi-underground blister hangar dug into the earth. But the wingspan was too great and she just wouldn't fit. That was a bloody good start, he thought. Then Ibby Waud arrived full of praise for his marvellous new machine which he said was an absolutely super aircraft, sweet as a nut and beautifully trimmed from the word go.

Most of the other pilots of 81 Squadron were chuckling about something and Wag overheard one of them say, 'Did you know, chaps, that they had a reception committee watching us come in? Loads of top Russian brass, I heard, and an Air-Vice-Marshal. That lot must have pissed themselves laughing when they saw the first Hurricane to land in Russia do a smart belly flop!'

It really was rather comic and Wag and Ibby were still laughing when a most antiquated little bus appeared and the driver beckoned them to get in. He was wearing a Russian naval uniform and smoking an enormously long Russian cigarette. Ibby pointed at the driver and said, 'Look, Wag, our first Russian. He seems casual enough!' Wag, of course, told the driver to take them to the dancing girls and off they drove on a hard and bouncy ride towards a squarish building surrounded by trees on the far side of the airfield. During the journey they could see Russian soldiers in the woods staring at them. 'I wouldn't like to meet that lot on a dark night', Wag whispered, and Ibby agreed. After clambering out of the bus they were told that they were going inside the building for a late breakfast.

The communal Mess was bright, spotlessly clean and immensely improved by Russian waitresses in gipsy skirts and blouses. Everybody was in good form when they sat down to a breakfast of cold Russian tea with raisins, a collation of meats, caviar, cheese, black bread and most surprising of all — quantities of Russian champagne. Champagne with breakfast had never been on any RAF menu and Ibby, who heartily approved of the innovation, raised his glass, 'Enormous cheers', he said to Wag and Nudger Smith on either side of him, 'here's to our Russian allies — God bless 'em!'

Wag thought that the Russians had put on a splendid show of welcome and it might be a fair idea to enjoy the breakfast champagne while it remained on the menu, as did the others. Nobody could tell whether Wing Commander Ramsbottom Isherwood approved or not because he never displayed any emotion, but Ibby Waud was prepared to lay bets that when the action started there would be no more early morning aperitifs.

After breakfast and in excellent spirits the pilots were taken by truck to their living quarters. Wag, Ibby and Nudger Smith shared a room which was bare except for the three beds. There was a hole in one of the walls covered by a tin flap which served as the fireplace for burning wood. Kitbags housed their personal gear and canvas bowls on wooden legs provided washing facilities. Water had to be got from a tap below and the 'loo' consisted of a hole in the ground with a plank. The living quarters, although somewhat primitive, were clean and fresh but it soon became obvious that visiting a Russian 'loo' was always going to be a most unsavoury experience.

The officers fared little better except that their building was a much more imposing two-storied structure in red brick surrounded by trees and looked like a large country house. Like the NCOs and airmen they had no running water and had to use canvas camp kit and the 'loos' smelt just the same! Upstairs the bedrooms were large and shared by three or four officers. There were no tapestries, trimmings or carpets and everything was basic, even the ante-room and bar. The ground floor served as Wing HQ and included an operations room, orderly rooms, sick quarters and stores. It wasn't long before the HQ was given a nickname and became known as 'The Kremlin'.

It took a day or two for the pilots to settle in and become accustomed to life on Russian soil in the autumn Arctic. The weather was cold but one didn't feel uncomfortable because it was a dry, crisp atmosphere and not a damp cold which permeates its way through the system. The vast airfield was a sandy earthy basin covering a frozen lake whose surrounds were quite muddy and marshy in places. It was totally unlike a typical RAF aerodrome in that the whole camp was hidden amongst hillocks covered by silver birch plantations. There were no highways except for one single metalled road running a mile through the isolated buildings and only rough paths and tracks connected one building or hut with another.

When Wag Haw had throttled back his Hurricane and put his flaps down to come in to land he was astonished at not seeing any hangars, buildings or anything reminiscent of a typical aerodrome. The whole set-up was scattered over a wide area, naturally camouflaged and well dug in. Hence it was less vulnerable to air attack but in other respects had its problems. Owing to the autumn rain and the heavy trucks the paths and tracks through the birch trees were full of pot-holes, axle deep in places. Also, it put a heavy strain on motor transport because aircrews and ground staff alike had to be carried over large distances backwards and forwards several times a day for meals and duties.

Wag Haw, Ibby Waud and Nudger Smith soon found that the Sergeants' Mess was a fair old walk through the woods from their living quarters. Ibby reckoned that it was well over half a mile but with gin at four shillings and sixpence a bottle the trudge was well worth while. There were Russian sentries posted outside both the living quarters and the Sergeants' Mess and strolling through the silver birches they noticed Russian soldiers with rifles lurking behind trees. It brought it home to them that the front line was only a few miles away and to an extent it was a comforting thought that hundreds of Russian marksmen had the place covered.

The Sergeants' Mess was a long wooden hut of the type used by the Germans in their prisoner-of-war camps. The furniture consisted of trestle tables, battered chairs and a bar at the far end. There were no refinements such as floor coverings and the place was double-skinned and heated by the usual wood-burning stove. But it provided the basic necessities of life including cheap booze, warmth and a place to congregate and relax.

Sitting drinking one evening shortly after they had arrived the three of them discussed their new situation. The Flight hut, a focal point in a fighter pilot's life, was on the eastern side of the airfield behind dispersals and turned out to be a very large dug-out. That day they had got their wind-up gramophone installed and the darts board fixed into position. The dozen or more records had survived the trip and it felt more like home to sit around there listening to the Ink Spots singing 'Whispering Grass' which was a favourite amongst the lads.

The tall, thin figure of Flying Officer McGregor suddenly appeared in the doorway and beckoned them outside. Mac pointed a finger towards the semi-buried earth blister hangars which had been too small to house their Hurricanes. Much to their astonishment they saw a Russian labour force shouldering picks and shovels emerging like an endless snake from the surrounding woods. Working like automatons they began digging out the hangars to make them wide enough to take a Hurricane's wing span. They worked without stopping for hours until the job was completed and then shouldering their picks and shovels they disappeared into the woods from whence they came. Nobody had any idea that there was a labour force on the camp and the whole thing appeared to be a mystery because there were so many of them and they had to be living somewhere. But the way they worked without stopping to take a breather or refreshment was an eye-opener to most pilots who made a mental note never to become involved in a Russian working party!

Vianga being a permanent Soviet airfield had surprised them because it was totally unlike anything that they had encountered in the RAF. Tony Rook had said that the Soviets had no radar system and that communications would be through the field telephone in Flights. There was no question, he emphasized, of them being vectored on to 'bandits' as they had been accustomed to at home but Russian ack-ack would undoubtedly point a finger at the Luftwaffe.

Ibby's only whispered comment to Wag was that everything will be marvellous as long as trigger happy Russian gunners concentrate on the Luftwaffe. 'But Wag, you bloody know that Ivan hasn't ever seen a Hurricane before — don't you?'

Neither had the British pilots come close to a Russian aircraft as yet. The blister hangars had been empty and there had been no sign of Russian bombers operating. The only indications of aerial activity were reports of enemy aircraft operating in the Murmansk area. Vianga had previously housed Soviet fighter squadrons but from the size of the blister hangars it was assumed that they must have been the old fashioned, barrel-like aircraft known as Ratas which had seen action in the Spanish Civil War. As was the case with the Luftwaffe when it attacked Russia, the British pilots had no idea how Russian aircraft performed or what they looked like.

Armourers had soon found out that they had a problem in that somebody had forgotten to include 'sears' when they packaged the gear at Leconfield. Consequently, it was only possible for them to get six machine-guns instead of the Hurricane's twelve operating. Home base was telegraphed and arrangements were being made to fly out the necessary 'sears' by a Catalina flying boat but it was going to take several days before they would arrive at Vianga. This was disappointing news for the pilots who had been looking forward to using the additional firepower, but it was not going to affect operational flying.

The British Hurricanes started operating from Vianga for the first time on 11 September. The programme was for pilots to familiarize themselves with the territory they were going to fly over and test their guns. Wag Haw found himself leading a section of three in vic formation on a day with broken cloud and good visibility. Flying east at 3,500 ft he could see the Murmansk Sound and the vague outline of the Rybachiy Peninsula known as Fisherman's Island. Down below, Murmansk itself looked like a shanty town. Three-quarters of it had been blitzed by the Luftwaffe but the buildings were wooden and therefore they didn't stand up in shattered outline like areas of London.

Having taken a look at the dock area and noted the rivulets and coastline Wag turned his section to port and made a sweep south and west. He wanted to avoid the Petsamo area which was dead ahead and where General Dietl and his Mountain Jägers were desperately trying to fight their way to the road leading to Murmansk itself. Although he had had no specific instructions to avoid combat he didn't wish to stick his neck out until he had some idea of the local geography. He knew from experience that mixing it in combat one loses all sense of location and direction and without radar he couldn't call up Vianga for a homing!

As they flew west the tundra countryside unfolded in a moving pattern of swamps, forests, lakes, peatbogs and glacial hills grey in colour and presenting a dreary landscape. Looking down as he gently weaved from side to side Wag thought what a bloody awful place it would be if he had to make a forced landing or bale out. There seemed to be no sign of human habitation for miles around, only a wilderness, and he shuddered to think what it would be like with the approach of a Russian winter. However, it was good to be back in the saddle again and feel the power of his 'jazzed up' Rolls-Royce engine running through his hands and the rhythmic motions of his Hurricane in flight as with fingertip control he performed gentle manoeuvres, playing with cloud formations.

It crossed his mind that they would have little trouble in navigating because all one had to do was to fly north and pick up the coastline just like they did on the South Coast back home or fly west and hit the Kola inlet. Visibility in the area so far had been remarkable and there were no mountains in the vicinity so even in bad weather they should be able to make base.

Having got the lie of the land and tested his guns Wag led his formation into a series of steep turns and gentle wing overs to loosen up. He wasn't going to do the giant stalls and fierce aerobatics as he did with Ibby because he didn't want somebody's propeller chewing off his wing tip. After an hour's flying which was thoroughly enjoyable he headed towards the airfield, glad to be back in the old routine once again.

Chapter 8
Action!

On the evening of 11 September the first snow of the year fell on their part of Russia and it looked as if the RAF Expedition might not have much time in which to operate. There had been a few light flurries of powdery stuff at Vianga and nobody knew whether this was a foretaste of things to come. The Russians told them that these flurries were unlikely to get heavier and more prolonged until late September and October, which would give them ample time to get some action.

The Wing was all geared to start offensive patrols and ready to escort Russian bombers on the following day and the general atmosphere that evening amongst pilots was that they were fit and 'raring to go'. There were still some technical problems for the engineer-officer's attention but Flight Lieutenant Gittins was still at the Keg-Ostrov aerodrome assembling the last Hurricanes which were to be flown into Vianga. The question of making fine adjustments to Merlin engines to compensate for the Russian low-octane fuel was one, and the other concerned the 'sears' necessary for installing six further machine guns to the aircraft giving them twelve-gun firepower.

The Expedition was still not complete because the Main Party with Flight Lieutenant Griffith, which was coming from Archangel by train, still hadn't arrived and had obviously been stuck or side-tracked somewhere *en route*. Throughout the Wing's stay in Russia a nightly signal was transmitted to Air Ministry by Wing Commander Ramsbottom Isherwood briefly giving details of the day's events. That night the usual signal went out but this time Isherwood reported that the Wing was primed and ready for action on the following morning.

Only six weeks had elapsed since Prime Minister Winston Churchill had telegraphed Premier Stalin to say that he was considering sending an RAF Fighter Wing to Murmansk. Even the rather dour and somewhat aloof Isherwood had to admit that to create a Wing, transport it to the Arctic Circle in the wilds of Northern Russia and be able to report that it was now operational after such a relatively short period was 'pretty good going by any standards'.

Visibility was very good on the following morning with about six tenths cloud at 5,500 ft. The first patrol was carried out by three aircraft from 134 Squadron who sighted enemy bombers but failed to make contact. An Me 110 was attacked and damaged on the second patrol by two aircraft from 81 Squadron. Later that morning 134 Squadron provided escort cover for Russian bombers on two occasions but there were no engagements.

Most of the officers of 81 Squadron had gone off in the trucks to the Mess for lunch leaving six pilots on readiness to form the usual two vic formations when they went into action. The pilots standing by included Wag Haw — the section leader — Jimmy Walker his number two, Ibby Waud, Nudger Smith and others. They were sitting around in their Mae Wests in the dispersal hut killing time and waiting for the field telephone to ring. It was a boring business, but one to which they were accustomed. It was impossible to really relax because they always had to have an ear cocked for the bell which might shriek out at any second.

Wag walked over to the gramophone which was crunching away at the end of the record and wound it up again. This time he shut his eyes and picked out a record blind from their collection of twelve. It turned out to be 'Julius Caesar' which was quite pleasant although they had all heard it hundreds of times. Big Ibby was leaning back in his chair with his great feet on a wooden box and appeared to be dozing but wasn't. 'For Chrissake, Wag', he called out, 'Can't you find something better than that bloody rubbish?'

Jimmy Walker was busy playing solitaire and Nudger Smith had gone outside for a pee, which was always a good move if one got the urge while on readiness. It could be quite painful to be caught short up in the air locked up in all those straps! Wag was keeping time with the music drumming his fingers on a trestle table as if he was playing the piano — which he sadly missed. The tune was one which brought back a vivid memory from the old Hendon days during the Battle of Britain.

Nudger Smith having accomplished his pre-action pee had just appeared in the entrance to the dug-out Flight hut when the bell of the field telephone rang out loud and clear. The section was to scramble and fly due west towards Petsamo where bandits were reported in the area. Pilots were told to look out for Russian flak bursts which would locate the German aircraft.

Wag ran out towards his Hurricane, tying the strings of his Mae West as he went. His ground crew were standing by with the accumulator trolley plugged in ready for him to press the starter button. The Merlin roared into life as he pulled on his helmet, plugged in his RT and oxygen and fastened his harness straps pulling them back tight. The engine was cold and his oil temperature gauge wasn't even showing a reading as, checking the other three Hurricanes on either side, he opened the throttle, leading the formation take-off.

His Hurricane rocked and bounced on the grey, uneven, sandy mud surface of the airfield until he gently pulled back on the stick and became airborne in smooth flight. Despite the cold engine his Rolls-Royce Merlin ran sweetly at full throttle without a cough or a hiccup. Climbing furiously he looked across at his chum Ibby and gave him the thumbs-up sign. He noticed that one of the chaps hadn't managed to get off the ground and that his formation consisted of only five Hurricanes but it didn't bother him. It felt great to be back in business again and he was excited as he watched the Kola inlet with its estuary widening out as they gained height.

Flying due west as ordered, he was about halfway between Murmansk and the coast, on his right. The sky was grey and overcast but the cloud base had lifted a little and he levelled out at about 5,500 ft searching for signs of Russian flak bursts. The surroundings were so grey and dull that he had to turn down the luminosity of his gunsight which had become almost dazzling. Visibility, however, was good and within minutes he caught sight of black powder puffs of Russian flak ahead and over to his right. Searching the air around the flak bursts he could see five black specks above the nose of his Hurricane flying across his sights from left to right. Yelling out 'Buster' to his formation over the RT he rammed his throttle wide open automatically turning his gun button to 'fire' as he climbed slightly, manoeuvring into position to attack the German aircraft.

As he got closer he could see five Me 109s which were escorting a Henschel 126, looking like an overblown Auster. Much to his astonishment the Germans turned away from the attacking Hurricanes. He could now see their black crosses quite plainly and the clipped wings of the Me 109E. He shouted 'Tally Ho' and dived on the nearest 109, delivering a quarter attack at close range. He hit the 109 underneath at its wing root and saw smoke and then fire belching out as he whipped his aircraft round in a hellishly tight right turn to lose speed and go after the Henschel but he was too late.

As Wag Haw went down on a 109, his chum Ibby Waud, leading blue section, had his eye on the Henschel. He described it later: 'A great deal happened in seconds. The damned fools turned away from us instead of turning in towards us. They must have been straight out of Operational Training Unit or maybe they'd been sent to the Russian front for being continually pissed. I was flying next to Wag as he opened fire on a 109. It burst into flames immediately, an appalling great ball of flame. I found myself catching up with Wag's 109 as it rolled over on to its back. It was an awesome sight, the 109 drifting along inverted with flames and debris pouring out of it. Black crosses, flames and smoke, one could almost smell them. The pilot must have been dead in the cockpit.

'As the flamer disappeared from my sight — this all taking seconds — the Henschel somehow drifted across my gunsight, right to left. Such a pretty little aeroplane but plastered with black crosses all the same, and instinctively I locked on to him and fired a short burst from the quarter. Another damn fool pilot, this one; he turned prettily, stuffed his nose down and dived very steeply towards the west; he must have been in a panic to get away, but he did quite the wrong thing in diving down in a dead straight line. He could have turned that Henschel in little circles on a pfennig and if he had done that, I wouldn't have had a chance of getting him. As it was, he presented a perfect 100 per cent dead astern target. Diving after him, I had a tremendous overtaking speed, but I opened fire and kept the button pressed all the way in. As I closed in, a huge plume of white smoke poured out of him (God, did I do that?). I passed over the top of him with what seemed like inches to spare, drawing in my breath in near-horror because I nearly collided with him.

'I immediately abandoned any interest in the Henschel, pulled the stick hard back and opened up the throttle to maximum. I was concerned with the main action — the 109s above me — and

ПРОПУСК № 42

Для прохода-проезда на аэродром,

Мурманск и Полярное

Фамилия   WAUD

Звание   SERGEANT PILOT

Нач. Штаба ВВС СФ

Above and below   *Sergeant Ibby Waud's Russian pass.*

Действителен

по „   1194   г.

Нач. Штаба ВВС СФ

Продлен

по „   194   г.

Нач. Штаба ВВС СФ

ГМ 14027   Зак № 4023

Left *Two Soviet matelots being offered cigarettes by an unidentified pilot of 134 Squadron.*

Below *81 Squadron pilots on the bonnet of their Ford estate wagon.*

Right *The cockpit of the clipped wing Me 109E — the main adversary!*

Left *Tony Rook, the CO of 81 Squadron, with Mac after a sortie.*

Below *In the hands of the skilled pilot the Me 109E was a formidable foe.*

Right *Wing Commander Ramsbottom Isherwood AFC accepts a light from Major General Kutzenov, who was a particularly good friend of the Expedition.*

Below *Ground crews pose for the picture around a Hurricane wrapped up in its Russian-made bedding against the cold.*

Above *Football in the snow as a Flight of Hurricanes take off overhead to escort Russian bombers.*

Below *The icy finger of the Murmansk winter.*

Above   *A Wing pilot steps out of the office after a successful sortie.*

Below   *Scrambling from dispersal.*

Above *Wag Haw and Ibby Waud talk to the Russian ace Sakarov.*

Left *Russian pilots fraternizing with British ground crews.*

clambered back to regain height and rejoin the party. But where was it? I looked around almost desperately, but could see no aircraft at first. I saw a Hurricane and a 109 circling round each other in classical combat style. I had the advantage of height and speed and was determined to keep it. Then began a cat-and-mouse game of diving down to attack the 109 and pulling up to superior height again.

'I started the first attack immediately and probably too hastily; the 109 might have had a chance to fire at me as I passed over him for the first time. But I made myself a difficult target. Thrashing both the engine and my own guts, I pulled up sharply again to regain height, twisting like a snake in the cockpit to keep the 109 in view. Then a second dive, and a second burst of fire at him, this time from the front quarter. Again I climbed and turned sharply, nearly screwing my eyes out of their sockets to keep the 109 in sight and make sure I still had the advantage. This combat was now taking an uncomfortably long time. Then suddenly the 109 broke away sharply to make a run for home, and made off towards the west. I still had the height over him and kept him carefully in view as he flew along the bed of a dried-up river, right down at nought feet and going like a bat out of hell. I positioned myself carefully above and behind him. Surely he could now see me coming? But he didn't deviate and once again I was presented with a perfect target from dead astern.

'Steadily overtaking, I put the red dot of my gunsight on the centre of the 109 and fired continuously all the way in. Why the hell didn't he turn around towards me? Flying straight and level, he was now signing his own death warrant. But he just kept on going, flat out (and desperate to get away, I imagine).

'As I closed in, I saw a thin stream of black smoke starting to pour from him. He veered to the left — not a proper turn, he just skidded away, left wing down a little — and crashed right into the bank of the river. There was a tremendous flash under my port wing as he exploded on the ground. It was yet another awesome spectacle.

'Once again, I immediately opened up to maximum revs and climbed to regain height, twisting around to look for other aircraft. I was still obsessed with the thought that there could be 109s above me, but for some time I saw nothing. But then, right ahead of me, a little dot, an aircraft twisting and turning like myself and at the same height. Was it a 109? I flew towards it and soon realized (with some relief) that it was a Hurricane. It turned out to be Wag!'

Having shot down a 109 and seen Ibby's Henschel veering away belching smoke Wag Haw had become locked in combat with another Messerschmitt. This developed into a cut and thrust affair ending up with vicious steep turns which in reality were controlled high-speed stalls in which the pilot is under great pressure. Neither could get a bead on the other and eventually the 109 broke away and dived for home. It was then that Wag saw a Hurricane trailing smoke and gradually losing height heading towards the Kola inlet in the direction of Vianga. He dived down towards it to take a look and saw that it was poor old Nudger Smith. There was a gaping hole behind the cockpit and the explosion must have jammed the hood because Nudger couldn't get out. He could see him wrestling with the canopy but was forced to break away and climb towards a 109 circling above.

When they had identified one another Wag and Ibby exchanged a few words over the RT. Then somehow Ibby lost sight of him and the sky was apparently empty again. He thought that Wag must have made off to base and so he did the same. He was conscious of the tension which had built up inside him and found that his legs were jumping and twitching uncontrollably on the rudder bar. As he switched off after landing, Ibby reflected for the first time that his Rolls-Royce Merlin engine had been well and truly thrashed and must have been nearly melting. He didn't jump down to the ground in his usual style but more or less slid down because his legs were like jelly. There were a lot of people around asking questions, but as soon as he could Ibby jelly-wobbled over to the semi-underground Flight hut and threw himself on one of the bunk beds and closed his eyes. Wag was there, doing the same.

*　　*　　*

Ginger Carter, his chum John Mulroy and the dozen other Hurricane pilots enjoyed the vodka and caviar party given to them by the Russian officers at Keg-Ostrov. The language barrier had done nothing to dampen the atmosphere in which sign language and raising glasses were all that mattered. Flight Lieutenant Micky Rook who was going to lead the formation to Vianga aerodrome had warned those unused to strong liquor to go easy on the vodka. 'We don't want anybody to prang on take off in front of our Russian audience!' he had said laughingly.

There was no doubt in any of the pilots' minds that the assembly operation at Keg-Ostrov had been an unqualified success. The general bonhomie and goodwill created between the Russians and Flight Lieutenant Gittins' 'Erection Party' was evident whenever pilots had left the liner to come and test the aircraft. Now all the Hurricanes were ready to depart and Gittins' job had been completed so no excuse was needed for a 'send off'.

Ginger Carter was a little apprehensive of the trip they were about to make. Vianga was some 300 miles to the north-west and this distance was near the limit of endurance for a Hurricane. Gittins' team had set the carburettors for maximum economy of fuel and stripped out the guns and ammunition but Carter was well aware that he would have to go easy on the throttle, keeping station in formation.

Flight Lieutenant Micky Rook explained when he briefed them that a Russian bomber was going to head the formation so there would be no problems regarding navigation or identity when they flew over Russian naval and ground forces. Visibility was good and there was about eight-tenths cloud at 6,000 ft when they took off from Keg-Ostrov. The first Hurricanes off had to circle the 'drome for some ten minutes or more while the others joined up forming a large 'V' behind the Russian bomber.

As they flew over the White Sea ships in the vicinity pooped off 'Very' lights and the Russian bomber responded with the colours of the day. They had been told that Russian forces throughout the area were very trigger happy and had expected anti-aircraft shells but fortunately none were forthcoming, despite the firework display.

After half-an-hour Ginger Carter discovered to his horror that he had been flying with a certain amount of skid on the aircraft by subconsciously using his left rudder and right aileron. It gave him a shock because the drag induced meant that he had been using more fuel than necessary, especially as they were using very low octane petrol supplied by the Russians. Looking down he could see that the landscape was more desolate than anything he had ever encountered and there was no sign of any human habitation. The interior was a pattern of rivers, lakes and scrub and any forced landing would mean certain death.

The thought of it made him continually trim his aircraft to avoid drag and he couldn't help himself glancing at his petrol gauges with monotonous regularity. When the formation was approaching Vianga he spotted the odd Hurricane darting about way ahead of them and wondered what the boys were up to, not realizing then that his Squadron had just shot down four of the enemy. It gave him a great sense of relief when he caught sight of the vast elongated airfield because only then was he sure that he had finally 'made it'. Even when he was coming in to land they gave him a red flare which made his heart miss a beat or two because he was practically out of juice but it was only a signal to make him land further down the 'drome.

Wag Haw entered the circuit just as the last of Micky Rook's formation landed feeling exhausted but pleased with himself after getting a 109. He knew that his section had bagged the Henschel and probably one or two other 109s and it had been a good show. They had been bloody lucky, he thought, to have been on readiness at that time and the officers who had pissed off to lunch would be kicking themselves.

The Canadian, Pilot Officer Jimmy Walker, had also bagged a 109 which made the score three Me 109s confirmed and one Henschel 126 probably destroyed for the loss of Nudger Smith. It took some time being debriefed and making out combat reports and then there was a chance to relax when the pilots were put on thirty minutes readiness. Wag was pleased to lie down not only because his knee was twitching a little after the excitement but also because he felt physically tired. Turning to Ibby, who had put his feet up alongside, he remarked that in his opinion a few minutes' dogfight was the equivalent of a weeks's hard labour. 'Those steep turns', he said, 'and throwing the aircraft around the sky. It's bloody hard work!'

Ibby grunted, not wanting to converse. All he wanted to do was to lie down because he felt completely 'knackered' and elated at the same time. He kept thinking about the 109 pilot whom he had shot down and recalled fragmentary glimpses of him during the dogfight and when he crashed in that remote valley. He had felt sorry to see him go down and wondered what sort of chap he had been. Probably like himself, he thought, mesmerized by the aerial battles over the Somme during the First World War and trying to relive those times.

Even Wag fell quiet and lay staring at the ceiling, oblivious to his surroundings and the crackly noises from the gramophone. Ibby's exhaustion gradually drained out of him and he could sense his vitality coming back. He was confident that his Henschel 126 would be confirmed because there was no chance that the little fat machine could ever have made base. It suddenly came home to him that he had shot down two German aircraft in his first dogfight over Russia. That was big stuff in anyone's language and he found it intensely rewarding because that had been his reason for joining the RAF in the first place.

Wag too, soon regained his natural exuberance and told Ibby that he still found it incredible that those Germans had turned slightly away from them when they had obviously seen the Hurricane formation. 'The stupid bastards must have thought we were Messerschmitts', he said, 'because otherwise they would have turned into us. They were obviously going fairly slowly to escort the Henschel which isn't a very quick machine,' he added, 'but they should have had the sense to 'break' not knowing for certain who we were.'

Ibby remarked that he was bloody glad that they hadn't. 'Those German pilots must have crapped themselves when they saw British Hurricanes with RAF markings coming down on them', he said. Going over the events, they were both bloody sorry that poor old Nudger Smith had bought it. Wag told Ibby that he had flown alongside Nudger and seen that the side of his aircraft had been shot away before he finally crashed. They figured out that it must have been Nudger who had been circling the 109 which Ibby had dived on and chased up the valley. Nudger, like themselves was a Yorkshire lad — from Leeds — though not a pre-war VR. He was too young for that, being only nineteen when he was killed and Ibby supposed that he should have been glad that he shot down the 109 who got Nudger. But he didn't feel like that at all, only sorry for both of them.

Later that day aircraft of 134 Squadron took off on the sixth patrol and intercepted three enemy bombers escorted by four Me 109s on their way to attack Archangel. The bombers immediately dropped their load without causing any damage and the enemy formation evaded combat. It had been a busy and successful day for 151 Wing and Wing Commander Ramsbottom Isherwood took great pleasure in signalling the Air Ministry that evening giving details of the day's actions.

*   *   *

The Wing Adjutant, Flight Lieutenant Hubert Griffith, and his party, consisting of about one hundred headquarters staff, had still not arrived at Vianga. Griffith's story continues from 7 September, when he was given his 'Movement Order' while still on board the *Llanstephan Castle* in dock at Archangel.

It sounded crazy to him when he read that his party would move provisionally on that day — but nobody knew whether the train to take them to Murmansk and on to Vianga would be ready that day or next Tuesday fortnight. They were told that the journey was expected to take from two to three days but could possibly take six days or more. It looked rather ominous when they were given a week's ration for luck — a week's ration for a journey of only 300 miles as the crow flies! He regarded this distance as being equivalent to a rail journey from London to Carlisle and it wasn't until he saw the map and was briefed by the Russians that he began to understand why they drew so much food.

For the first part of the journey he could see that the train would be heading south on the Archangel/Moscow line. Then at a junction which appeared to be in the middle of nowhere, as far as he could make out on the map, the train turned west following the coastline of the White Sea. The Russians said that this link line was a single line track which had been recently laid across 200 miles of sandy soil finally connecting up with the Leningrad-Kandalaksha-Murmansk railway at a place named Belomorsk. The train would then head north, they told him, still hugging the coastline of the White Sea, until it reached Kandalaksha when it wriggled around lakes until it finally got to Murmansk. The total distance was some 600 miles and not the 300 that he had anticipated.

The train eventually pulled out of Archangel with everybody packed into two rugged passenger coaches with no refinements whatsoever except plain deal boards to stretch out on. There were only enough straw palliasses for half the men so it was going to be a question of drawing lots or taking turns when they 'kipped down' for the night. Griffith did the decent thing allowing a Sergeant and a batman to share his compartment and refusing the luxury of a palliasse, saying that he never minded a touch of discomfort.

They found the landscape extremely dull and monotonous with nothing but sand dunes, hillocks and stunted birch trees. Grey, low, heavy clouds hung menacingly over the area and the temperature was equivalent to late English autumn weather, coolish but quite reasonable. Supper that night consisted of bully beef and bread which went down well but those sleeping on bare deal boards found life rather hard after the comfort of the liner.

Griffith woke up the next morning feeling as if he had been stretched on a rack and for a moment regretted his decision to set an example and do without the straw. After a night on them those deal boards seemed to get harder and harder as though they were

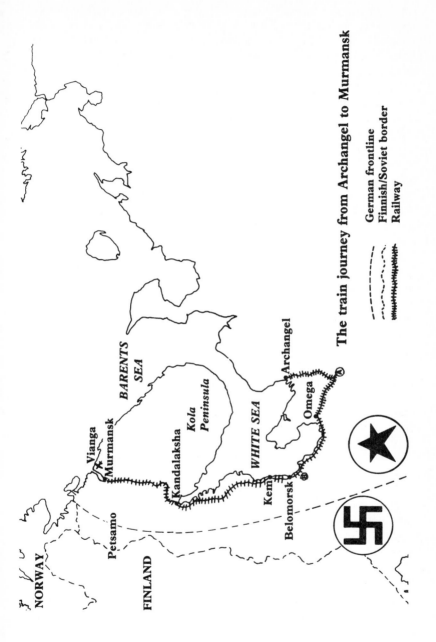

The train journey from Archangel to Murmansk

German frontline
Finnish/Soviet border
Railway

NORWAY

BARENTS
SEA

Vianga
Murmansk
Petsamo

FINLAND

Kola
Peninsula

Kandalaksha

WHITE SEA

Kem

Belomorsk

Omega

Archangel

made of immortal ebony but he wasn't going to give in and ask for a palliasse. Tinned stew, heated over spirit cookers, provided lunch while at odd intervals the train pulled into a siding or wayside station when Russian railway officials would clamber aboard with large cans of boiling hot water for tea making.

By this time the train had transferred on to the single line track and was heading west along the coastline of the White Sea through a landscape of firs, pines and the inevitable low hills. The maximum speed was only a little faster than a brisk walking pace and for light in the late evenings there were a couple of candles stuck in the corridor outside each compartment.

They halted for about an hour opposite a Russian hospital train coming down the line that afternoon and Griffith was able to try out his Russian which he had been trying to learn in England during recent years. Much to his astonishment he found that he got on very well in understanding them and being understood. This chance meeting in the wilderness of the tundra country had all the air of a reunion about it when Griffith told them that 'we are the RAF arriving'. Russian soldiers in slings and bandages gave the universal thumbs-up sign and were obviously in good spirits despite the fact that the Germans were advancing on all fronts. Cigarettes and sweets were exchanged amongst the troops while the Russian nurses in white overalls looking very clinical and efficient gave wide grins.

Nobody took their clothes off at night because they provided padding against the hardness of the deal boards and washing was a luxury. A little cold water in a mug had to suffice for the odd shave while the hot water which the Russians unfailingly provided was used to make the strong, sweet tea which all airmen adore.

Occasionally, Russian troops boarded the train and one evening Griffith was invited into a compartment shared by two Russian Colonels together with a batman and a minor train official. They were in their late thirties and looked smart giving the impression that they only had to issue an order and everyone would come running. After drinking Russian tea the party went on late into the evening during which one of the Colonels, acting as chef, heated up tins of soup by holding them with his fingers over a candle. Conversation flowed freely throughout that midnight candlelit tea party without any restraint and Griffith recorded that 'one could see the complete friendliness that existed between them all — each member of the party saying all he thought, discussing the situation freely and without constraint, cracking jokes, just as though ranks between Colonels and batmen did not exist.' Griffith was an enthusiast undoubtedly because of his pre-war interest and visits to Russia. The free-for-all situation which he had experienced in the compartment throughout the candlelit party was something that in his opinion the Russians had achieved in the last twenty years and he doubted whether we in the UK had ever thought of emulating it. It showed, he said, among other things that Afinogenov's play 'Distant Point' dealing with the relationship between high Soviet officers and their subordinates was no lie. He was particularly pleased to find this out from personal experience because he had translated the play from the Russian several years previously.

Further down the single track line they met another hospital train where there was a repeat performance highlighted by one of the airmen having his tunic button sewn on by a Russian nurse with a crowd of about a hundred Russians watching and applauding. When they reached Belomorsk the train linked up with the Leningrad-Kandalaksha-Murmansk railway and headed north, still following the coastline of the White Sea until they reached Kandalaksha right at the northern top of an inlet. They had already crossed the Arctic Circle north of Loukhi and were now heading into the Kola Peninsula. Murmansk was then about 150 miles away and virtually due north but the train had to turn east for some thirty or forty miles, skirting round the lakes in the area of Kirovsk and making the journey seem endless.

By the fourth day out Griffith was aching all over but doing his best to put it out of his mind by telling himself that it was all part of the hardening-up process. While he was eating breakfast of herrings out of a tin and swilling hot sweet tea he remembered the events of the previous evening. Early in the journey the Russians had given the airmen a concertina or a 'garmonica' as they called it and this had rarely stopped playing. The previous night a couple of young Russian officers had boarded the train and hearing the old squeeze box going full blast had joined the airmen. Neither of them could speak a word of English but music is a universal language and they began singing operatic airs accompanied by the 'squiffer', which got everybody going.

When the train finally pulled into Murmansk at midday there was a great deal of excitement on board. The long journey was nearing its end and the camp was only seventeen miles away. It was going to be a relief to get off the train and minds conjured up visions of hot baths and a change of clothing. But life moves at its own pace in Russia and they were shunted about the sidings for two hours before setting off on the last lap.

This last stretch was accomplished by a small puffer locomotive which pushed the train backwards up a steep winding track. It chugged its way for nearly four hours stopping now and again to relax and take a breather. Finally at about four o'clock in the afternoon it arrived at Vianga airfield which everybody noted was buried in the remotest countryside and appeared to be miles away from any form of civilization.

Griffith and his party had been very lucky to have completed the trip without incident. German bombers and fighters were very consistently attacking targets in the Kola Peninsula particularly in the Murmansk and Archangel areas. Rail links allowing the Russians to bring reinforcements and supplies to the front line were prime targets and railway lines were often under repair from bombing attacks. By western standards the Murmansk railway system was old fashioned, slow and totally unpredictable. Yet it enabled the Russians to carry on throwing in reserves and so contain the advance of General Dietl.

To have come by train from Archangel, which is about the same latitude as Reykjavik in Iceland, on a journey of some 600 miles across the Arctic Circle to the port of Murmansk was an experience shared by few other Englishmen. For the RAF party it had been a journey of a lifetime and one which none of them would ever forget. They alone among the 550 men comprising the Expedition had had the opportunity of a close look at the wild and desolate region surrounding the White Sea and in the hinterland of the Kola Peninsula. Furthermore, they had come into close contact with Russian forces and learned something of their style and approach to life.

Perhaps the most remarkable aspect of the trip was the friendliness and obvious goodwill displayed by the Russians whom they encountered way out in the wilds. The hospital trains certainly gave the airmen an insight into the Russian character. They were surprised to see wounded Russian soldiers on their way back from the front singing and waving regardless of the fact that the war had been going very badly for them. Everyone appeared to be cheerful, usually sporting a wide grin and willing to fraternize.

With the arrival of the Wing Headquarters Party under Griffith the entire Wing was at last at full strength. While getting themselves organized after the train journey the arriving party heard the news that the Wing had just been in action and that four Huns had been shot down for the loss of one Hurricane. This gave everybody from 'erk' to station commander a tremendous uplift and sense of pride. There was no question at Vianga or later that night at the Air Ministry in London that 151 Wing had got off to a splendid start in their Russian adventure.

Chapter 9
The bridge at Petsamojoki

The battle along the Petsamo front in Northern Russia had increased in its ferocity. Dietl's Mountain Jägers had reached the new road to Murmansk and on the left wing regiments of his 2nd Mountain Division had cleared out the Russian 58th Rifle Regiment from the high ground along the 'Long Lake' in the area of the Gulf of Kola, along the shore of which stands the port of Murmansk.

Stukas, in their role as forward artillery, strongly supported these attacks but the Siberian troops took full advantage of the rocky terrain and made difficult or almost impossible targets to eliminate. Both sides suffered heavy losses in close combat battles but when things appeared to be going well for the Germans the Soviets mounted counter attacks fed by local supply bases and the advance ground to a halt.

The Germans had failed to put the Murmansk Railway out of action and 'Operation Platinum Fox' — the code name given to the drive to capture Murmansk — was stuck at the entrance to the new road with the town and port only twenty miles or so away. It was clear that General Dietl needed more divisions and supplies back-up to break through the Siberian counter-onslaught. He had already suffered heavy casualties crossing the River Litsa and as the Soviets hurled wave after wave of Siberian troops at him he was beginning to feel that he might be compelled to withdraw behind that cursed river of the Arctic tundra.

The German General realized that time was running out and

within a matter of weeks the Russian winter would be just around the corner. He kept on recalling Hitler's words when they had discussed the North Russian campaign. 'You've got to manage those ridiculous sixty miles from Petsamo to Murmansk with your Mountain Jägers', the Führer had said. Dietl knew that if only Hilter had given him more divisions and allowed him to concentrate his forces on taking Murmansk he would be in that garrison town with its port and supplies depot by now. He had been obliged to accept a compromise and now he was facing the inevitable consequences of not having enough power and back-up in any one area to do the job.

A few days previously on 9 September the British Navy had attacked his supply ships just off the coast along from Murmansk and supplies had now become a major problem. Even when they arrived they had to be manhandled by his labour force across this dreadful terrain on their way up to the front line. Dragging horse-drawn guns through the swamps, rocks and scrub and up steep inclines had been an agonizing and back-breaking business. Dietl had also been forced to employ two thirds of his men on supplies leaving him short in the combat area. By contrast, the Russians brought up reinforcements of men and supplies by road right up to the battlefield.

When Dietl's forces did make ground, the Soviets were able to play the numbers game and employ non-stop counter attacks. Such continual pressure, often in hand-to-hand fighting situations when the Siberians kept on coming at them with total disregard for being mown down, meant that the Germans eventually ran short of ammunition and were compelled to go on to the defensive.

*   *   *

Although the airfield at Vianga was attacked spasmodically by the Luftwaffe there was no immediate danger of it being overrun. It was reported that the nearest Germans were at least fifteen or more miles away and the airfield was well guarded, with Russian soldiers hidden in the surrounding woods. The airmen were told that these Russian forces were there to deal with any German patrol ferreting behind the lines or escaping prisoners-of-war — who in Russia had a short life expectancy!

The Hurricane pilots who had just flown in from the Keg-Ostrov airfield outside Archangel were busy getting themselves organized with accommodation and 'doing the rounds'. They had chosen a good moment to arrive because everybody was remarkably cheerful and excited about the four Huns that had just been shot down. Like Wag Haw and Ibby Waud, however, when they had first arrived on the airfield, Ginger Carter and his chum John Mulroy were astonished by the haphazard, scattered and disjointed layout of the camp. Muddy rough paths or tracks with pot-holes axle-deep in slush led through the woods leading from one building to another. They soon discovered that the dining halls were about one third of a mile from the living quarters and it was going to be a long walk from the billet to the Sergeants' Mess!

They had to trudge almost half a mile from their sleeping quarters through stark and stunted silver birches before arriving at the headquarters building known as 'The Kremlin'. Checking in at the orderly room they wandered down a bare corridor and by chance found an 'Operations Room' with the familiar ops boards fixed as usual to the walls. Looking hard at the blackboards displaying aircraft number, letters, names, Flights and squadrons, John Mulroy turned to Ginger and remarked that this was the only damned corner of Vianga which reminded him of a typical RAF station.

That evening they had their first real taste of Russian food after enjoying the cuisine on board the liner for some three weeks. The scenario, with the Russian waitresses buzzing about, was certainly an 'eye opener' and so was the supper which included smoked salmon, caviar, vegetable soup, rather tough goose and preserved plums served in a glass with syrup. There was no booze served during the meal which didn't seem to make any difference because the atmosphere was good humoured and everybody seemed to be enjoying themselves. Ginger Carter was surprised to learn that the Russian staff had to cater for five sittings for every meal. As there were over 500 airmen this was hardly surprising, but senior NCOs had their own special sitting. The officers and NCOs were given similar food and large decanters of rich red wine were placed on tables at the evening meal.

The story went around that an HQ officer had suggested to the manageress of the Russian staff that the airmen should bring their own knives, forks, spoons and mugs as they did at home. This was a well-meaning gesture intended to save the Russians a vast washing up programme in between sittings but she ignored it for several days. When approached again she flatly refused the offer saying that guests should not have to bring their own mugs and eating utensils to the table. Her argument was difficult to understand, especially as she was a member of a Communist regime which one would have thought would have welcomed the idea as part of its own philosophy. Quite apart from that the resultant faster turnover at meal sittings would have helped the operational flying programme which had to be carried out at all costs. Perhaps it was one of the anomalies of the regime but as Griffith recorded, 'at least it indicated an extreme of zeal, cooperative willingness and hospitality'. Nobody knew whether their Russian counterparts brought their 'mugs and irons' with them to meals and washed them afterwards because Soviet Messes were miles away in the environs of the airfield and were a closed shop as far as the RAF was concerned.

When the newly-arrived Ginger Carter and John Mulroy settled into their brick-built sleeping quarters they found them infested with vermin. John was forced to shave off his hair and, not wishing to go around looking like a boiled egg, he wound bandages around his head. For a man who was highly conscious of his appearance and who had had his uniform tailor-made it was a 'lousy' experience. Ginger was friendly with the transport chief who had also come from the Midlands and the chap had had a wooden hut built from crates which had carried equipment. So they moved into his quarters which were comfortable and more like home. It was very bad luck that they happened to choose one of the two rooms in the entire barrack blocks which had to be fumigated. This was also the case with some older outbuildings of wooden construction just beyond the boundaries of the camp. The Wing had taken them over to serve as Sergeants' Mess, airmen's recreation room and store houses. Old wooden huts apparently were a notorious problem and these had been occupied by a succession of labour forces who had been brought in to build the camp and the strongest measures had had to be employed to de-bug them.

The funeral of Sergeant Nudger Smith took place on 14 September on a dull overcast day when there was hardly any flying. It is an emotional experience for most fighter pilots who have to attend the funeral of one of the brethren and Wag Haw and Ibby Waud who were to be pallbearers could only regard it as a duty which they had to perform. Nudger had always promised that if he ever went down he would come back from the dead and give them a nudge in the arm, as he used to do in life with his knuckles. While they were smartening themselves up before climbing into the back of the three-tonner Wag laughingly gave Ibby a dig in the ribs and made a joke about Nudger. Ibby who was looking very

Above *The close liaison between RAF and Soviet personnel led directly to the incredible success of the Expedition.*

Right *Having handed their Hurricanes to the Russians, tobogganing became a major pastime.*

146

Left *Skiing was a new art to be mastered for many!*

Below left *British air-technician Freeman trains Soviet pilot V. Maksimovich to fly a Hurricane.*

Right *A wartime publicity photograph of the Russian ace Colonel Sakarov.*

Below *Ibby Waud and Wag Haw discuss tactics with the Russian ace Sakarov as a Flight of Hurricanes formates above Vianga airfield.*

Overleaf *Publicity given to his son's activities in Russia resulted in Wag Haw's father receiving letters from factories, union officials and committees from all over the United Kingdom.*

147

12 Park Grove York

14th January, 1942.

Mr. F.T. Haw,
23 Fifth Avenue,
York.

Dear Mr. Haw,

At a meeting of the Electricity Committee held last Thursday mention was made of the distinctions your son has been awarded for his skill, courage, and devotion to duty in his service with the R.A.F. The Committee and I feel these awards are richly deserved and offer our heartiest congratulations to yourself and Mrs. Haw on your son's success.

We fervently hope he will be spared to enjoy the benefit of peace he has already done so much to bring about.

Yours faithfully,

C.T. Hutchinson

Chairman,
Electricity Committee, York Corporation.

serious told him to watch it saying, 'I should be careful if I were you, Wag. One of us might be next on the list.'

They clambered aboard the three-tonner in company with other Sergeants including Rigby and Avro Anson. Nobody said much as the truck rolled and bumped its way towards the road leading to the village of Vianga which was about a mile and a half from the camp. Wag, who had never been out of the camp, was gazing out of the back of the truck. As far as he could make out the village consisted of a couple of hundred wooden shacks with a few larger wooden buildings and some brick-built barracks. It looked rather drab and uninteresting as the truck passed through and headed towards Murmansk.

It took them nearly an hour before they finally arrived at a village on high ground overlooking the Murmansk Sound. Then they carried the coffin through the village and up to the grave with the British White Ensign which the Russians had made and dyed and the flag of the Soviet Fleet Air Arm draped side by side over it. Ibby was most moved by the occasion and saw old ladies with head scarves looking mournful and sad and Russian soldiers in fur hats saluting as the coffin passed them.

The RAF had a firing party and the Russians also sent one. It was a simple ceremonial affair with Flight Lieutenant Fisher reading the funeral service. Standing beside the grave and casting an eye over towards the still waters of the Kola inlet, Wag wished that a Hurricane had been detailed to come streaking across the landscape as a final salute. It would have been better that way, he thought.

Escorting Russian bombers attacking ground targets and carrying out reconnaissances in the Petsamo area was one of the prime functions of 151 Wing. When they began operations Hurricane pilots soon discovered that the Soviets had a twin engined machine with a considerable performance and they had to open throttles wide to maintain station.

These were Pe-2 and Pe-2 FT bombers which operated from a satellite of the main Vianga airfield. Both types had only recently been introduced into the Red Air Force and their high performance was achieved by clean lines and a high aerodynamic efficiency. The Pe-2 was designed as a light reconnaissance bomber and carried a crew of three or four depending on its assignment. It had a maximum speed of 300 mph and a bomb load of 1,700 lb and rapidly became one of the most widely used and efficient types of bomber in the Red Air Fleet. The Pe-2 FT was an improved version of the Pe-2, used as a dive-bomber and for low level ground attack work, as well as in the role of a light precision bomber. It could carry a maximum bomb load of 2,200 lb and its top speed was 335 mph at 16,000 ft making it a very useful machine indeed.

Except when they were on escort duty the Hurricane pilots saw nothing of the Russian bombers or their aircrews and ground crews who lived in a camp some distance away. Neither did they have any close contact with Russian fighters who were operating in the area. Ibby Waud had by some curious arrangement done a sector recce with a Russian fighter. 'It was a small, tubby, barrel-like machine', he said, 'with a bloody great red star painted on the side. It looked like a smaller version of the Thunderbolt to me and as we poodled along over the area the Russian pilot was grinning and waving his arm.' Ibby didn't know it at the time but his escort was undoubtedly an I-16, known as a Rata, which was still in service on the Eastern Front.

While on patrol on 17 September the Wing had another memorable day. Wag Haw had satisfied the inner man at lunchtime with the inevitable smoked salmon, caviar, some very good cold ham and fried eggs but was unable to manage the preserved fruit. The ham and fried eggs had gone down particularly well, being English-style food, and made a change from Archangel cutlets and other Russian meat dishes which were usually rather tough. This was the first time that they had had real eggs which were exceptionally tasty after dull and rubbery omelettes made with egg powder. He had shaken his head when the Russian waitress had made signs indicating that he could have another egg if he wanted but Ibby had given her the thumbs-up and was rewarded with another plate of *three* eggs!

The truck picked them up after lunch and bumped its way back along the rough track leading to their semi dug-in flight hut. The weather for a change was quite bright with the sun shining through gaps in the cloud instead of the usual grey blanket which made the whole scene dull and dreary. Wag thought how pretty the silver birch plantation looked with the sun coming through the trees reminding him of home.

Soon after the pilots walked down the steps into the Flight hut the field telephone announced a bomber escort job for 81 Squadron. Tony Rook would be leading the show and Wag found himself down to lead blue section with Avro Anson as his number two and Rigby as three. Squadron formation was to be the one they had developed and used during the Battle of Britain. Red section leading in a vic of three, blue and green sections in trailing vic formation behind red two and red three and yellow section as weavers with yellow one line astern of red leader and yellow two and three stepped above and below the formation. The idea of the weavers was to look out for bandits and protect the rear of the Squadron formation.

While they were lounging about word came through that the sears required for their additional machine-guns were now on their way by Catalina flying boat.

The idea of having twelve guns to blast away with was an exciting prospect for most of them but Wag had his doubts about the extra armament. He wondered how the machine would handle with the additional guns. One would be alongside the existing three and the other two halfway between the present guns and the wingtip. It would mean extra weight, he knew, but those guns nearer the wingtips would probably increase the turning circle and the Hurricane's ability to turn inside a Messerschmitt was one of its prime virtues. Facetiously, he said to Ibby that if a pilot couldn't hit anything with six guns then despite the wider arc and heavier density of fire he was unlikely to do any better with twelve. Ibby who was in a dozy state after his big lunch had his feet up on a wooden crate and wasn't going to be drawn. 'All I know, Wag', he said with a yawn, 'is that you are full of bullshit.'

Snoring off was all right for Ibby, he thought, Ibby wasn't going on the show that day which was probably the reason why he had stuffed himself at lunch. Looking at Ibby in a semi-comatose state reminded him that being stood down and having a day off was a boring business because there was nowhere to go and bugger all to do. It had always been tedious waiting for something to happen because one was unable to settle down to anything, have an ear half-cocked listening for the field telephone to ring.

Feeling a little closed in he went outside to sniff the air and take a breather. The generator was chugging away with the water wagon standing alongside. Scattered stunted birch trees crept up the little barren hillocks like the stubble of an unkempt beard. A lone Hurricane stood forlornly in front of a battered wooden stores hut in an area of slushy mud and puddles. Away to his left Wag could see ground crews manning a suction pump waggon in an attempt to drain a small lake which was creeping towards dispersals. Other ground crews getting the Squadron's aircraft ready for the show were plugging in 'acc' trolleys, wiping windscreens and checking the machines before take off. He stood there motionless looking at the clouds and the great basin of the airfield which stretched across the horizon. The weather was fresh but he didn't feel the cold wearing his Mae West like a padded waistcoat and in his battledress, thick grubby white polo neck jersey and heavy flying boots.

Standing looking across the airfield he found it difficult to believe that he was actually in Russia. He might well have been in Northern Scotland or Skye, he thought, except that there was no heather and nothing to soften the landscape. Only the sight of Russian waitresses and soldiers in fur hats and hearing the language brought it home to him. One or two of the pilots had already acquired fur hats as souvenirs and he laughed, picturing Ibby wearing one. The thought reminded him that he and Ibby were due to go into the village on the following day to have a look round and participate in a steam bath which promised to be a hilarious exercise. Ibby had been saying that the village looked like a cowboy town from the air and was just a row of wooden shacks as far as he could make out but at least they would be seeing something of the real Russia for the first time.

Wag's large lunch reminded him that he was due to pay a visit to the loo and he walked round the back of the Flight hut to the Russian version at dispersal. This consisted of a deep hole in the ground with a plank across it. There was a hole in the middle of the plank for practical purposes and although hidden from view there were no screens or protection from the elements and one simply had to perform out in the open. The one outside their living quarters was similar except that it was protected by a wooden hut and was known as the 'thunderbox'.

Everybody hated Russian loos because they stank and were messy affairs and Wag made his visits as short as possible, greatly assisted by the rich and oily food! Ibby's comments after a few excursions had been rather basic and down to earth. 'There's shit all over the place', he said, 'and the Russians have no bloody idea about sanitation.' Wag was particularly fortunate on this occasion to have carried out his bodily function because when he entered the Flight hut the field telephone was screeching out. It was answered as usual by Corporal Dixon who announced that bandits had been reported and the Squadron was to scramble and patrol the area around the Kola inlet.

Everything else was forgotten as pilots grabbed gear and ran out to their aircraft. Although being 'scrambled' had become almost a routine for Wag, it always had an electrifying effect upon him. Racing across to his Hurricane, taking a quick glance up at the sky, his mind and body had changed up into top gear as if somebody had injected him with some kind of super drug making him highly tuned and excited all at once.

His RAF training ensured that he could carry out his cockpit drill like an automaton and within seconds he waved away his chocks. The engine was cold and the needle of his oil temperature gauge hadn't even registered as he opened up the throttle for take-off, hoping that his Rolls-Royce Merlin would perform without any hiccups. Sensitive to his machine rocking from side to side as he rapidly gathered speed and the deafening roar from the engine he was glad to ease back on the stick and claw his way up into the smoother air.

He glanced across at Avro Anson on his left and Rigby on his right and waved them into line astern formation watching as they throttled back and disappeared to tuck their noses behind his tail. Slowly working the throttle he manoeuvred into position behind Red Two of the leading section as the Squadron formed up in battle formation.

With hands and feet automatically controlling his machine Wag was able to maintain station behind Red Two and fly by the seat of his pants. This enabled him to keep his head out of the cockpit and search the sky for any glimpse of a bandit. The Squadron climbed at full throttle to 5,000 ft levelling out below great chunks of heavy grey clouds whose tops sparkled in the sun. It was one of Russia's fine days and only the second during which the Wing had been able to carry out a full operational programme.

Down below on his right Wag could see the Kola inlet with shafts of sunlight bouncing off the water. Even the surrounding tundra landscape had lost its grey drab appearance where patches of sun highlighted lakes, marshes and scrub. Flying over the inlet high above the port of Murmansk and the town of Kola the Squadron turned to port and headed south, patrolling the border area of Petsamo.

There had been no sign of any Russian flak bursts to point a finger at bandits and Wag was beginning to think that the patrol would prove negative. Some of his earlier feelings of being 'keyed up' had dissipated as they patrolled up and down a line, screwing their heads round looking for business. Occasionally he glanced at his instruments but the needles were all stable in their rightful positions and his Merlin engine was running sweetly. Turning west into the sun he had just turned up his reflector gunsight when he saw tracer flashing past above and to the right of his starboard wing as an Me 109 from nowhere slowly passed him. Kicking on rudder and opening the throttle wide he closed in behind the bandit. He eased slightly back on the stick and had the German perfectly positioned in his sights. Pressing his gun button he fired a long burst and saw his shells hit the underneath of the German's wing root. The 109 spewed out white glycol vapour as he yanked back on the stick and using a touch of rudder hauled his Hurricane round in a split-arse climbing turn twisting his head for any sign of further bandits.

His heart was thumping and the 'g' force weighed heavily upon him pinning him down in his metal seat and making his arms and legs feel like lead. From the staccato crackle over the RT he knew that some of the others were having a ding-dong battle with other 109s. Peering down from his cockpit in the fierce spiral climb he could see the sunlit waters of a small lake revolving slowly and fading like a burned out comet as he broke into a blanket of grey swirling mist.

Uptight and unsure of himself he automatically concentrated on his instruments to keep the Hurricane flying straight and level. The sight of the tracer from that 109 flashing over his wingtip had shaken him to the core and even now his heart was still thumping away overtime. The 'g' forces had gone now that he was flying normally but his muscles were like tightly coiled springs and he forced himself to relax, unclenching his hands and waggling his toes. Having to fly by instruments for a few minutes did him good because when he throttled back and broke cloud he was more relaxed and confident.

It astonished him to find that the surrounding sky had been wiped clean of aircraft as he headed north to pick up the Kola inlet and make his way back to base. The Squadron had vanished within a few minutes and there was no sign of a bandit. He had a strange and eerie feeling that those few seconds of terror had never happened. His mind went back to the Battle of Britain when the sky appeared to be filled with bombers and yet within a minute or two of fierce combat he had found himself alone in a vast expanse of blue and searching for any trace of the action.

As the inlet came in sight again he realized how bloody lucky he had been. Those 109 pilots, he thought, must have nipped through a gap in the clouds and dived on them out of the sun. He knew that

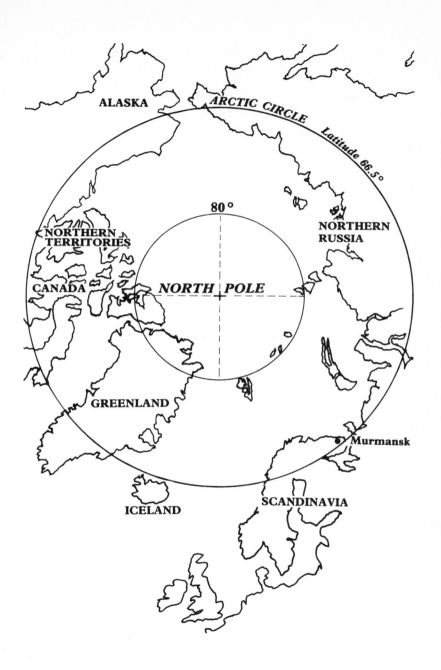

**Polar Projection, showing the position of
Murmansk within the Arctic Circle**

the German who had a go at him must have been an inexperienced pilot. The bastard had failed to shoot him down and then presented him with a perfect target which every fighter pilot dreams about. He couldn't believe it at the time when the 109 had slowly overtaken him about fifty feet above and then continued to fly straight and level. All he had to do was to cock his nose up and shoot the bugger down. The realization that he must have knocked down a second 109 acted like a tonic and made him feel good. Taking a quick look inside the cockpit to check that everything was in order he turned the world upside down and aerobatted his way home in high spirits.

Coming in on the approach to landing he took a closer look at the village of Vianga. Ibby was right, he thought, the place did look like a small Wild West wooden shanty town — the kind of film set used for cowboy movies — although he noticed one or two more solid looking buildings and thought that one of them might house the steam bath which they were going to sample. He pushed flap down and he made a curved approach using his throttle to ensure that he touched down well up the airfield. The three-and-a-half ton machine sank gently onto the rough sandy uneven surface rocking from side to side and giving a little grunt or groan now and then as the oleo legs of the undercarriage took the strain. His ground crew looked up rather expectantly as he taxied into dispersal giving the engine a final burst and then throttling back and switching off.

His watch told him that he had been airborne for 45 minutes as he unclipped his oxygen mask and pulled off his helmet and gloves. His mouth was dry and the cold air refreshing as he breathed in great gulps before jumping down off the mainplane and stretching his arms and legs as if he had just rolled out of bed. Nobby, his engine fitter, walked over, carefully balancing a mug of hot sweet tea which he handed to him. Then his armourer and rigger joined them and the three airmen watched him expectantly as he swallowed a mouthful of the deliciously reviving brown liquid before giving them a thumbs-up sign. They knew immediately that he had bagged another one and Nobby gave him a fatherly pat on back of his Mae West as he made his way, mug in hand, to the Flight hut.

The place was buzzing with excitement — a sure sign that it had been a good show. His number two, Sergeant Avro Anson, clapped him on the back and told him that he had confirmed the Me 109 he had attacked. 'I thought he'd got you at first, Wag, because his tracer was that damn close. Then you really clobbered him and I saw him go down. Bags of white smoke and then the black stuff as he spun in.' In the midst of the gathering he overheard Ginger Carter talking to his chum John Mulroy and heard him say, 'Old Wag Haw always seems to be in the right place at the right time. I saw him pull his nose up and knock down that 109 — he's a dead-eyed dick all right!'

The Intelligence officer was busy de-briefing other pilots and Wag, having a touch of the 'knee trembles', sat down waiting for his turn to describe the action and fill in his official combat report. The Squadron had shot down four Me 109s without loss on the patrol which ignited the atmosphere inside the Flight hut, although understatement was the name of the game. Wag's reply to some of the pilots who came up to congratulate him was typical. 'All I had to do was to press the tit. The 109 was sitting in my gunsight flying straight and level. Piece of cake, really.' Of course they referred to him as 'that lucky bastard Haw' but underlying the jocularity they were well aware that the cobby little Flight Sergeant was making a name for himself on the Russian Front.

⋆　⋆　⋆

Prime Minister Winston Churchill had made it perfectly clear to Premier Stalin that the fighter aircraft which Britain had despatched to Northern Russia had seriously diminished reserves although compared with the losses sustained by the Red Air Force the gesture might appear to be a petty one. On 15 September Stalin had telegraphed Churchill saying that in the absence of a second front he would like some thirty British divisions to be sent to Archangel or transported through Persia to fight in the southern regions.

This request in Churchill's view was quite ludicrous and in the realms of the absurd. Beaverbrook was sent on a mission to Moscow to reassure Stalin that aid for Russia was of prime importance but some things were impossible. Among other things, Churchill said that the mission could offer Stalin Britain's entire tank production for the week ending 27 September. Churchill pointed out that on 16 September RAF bombers had attacked military and industrial installations in Hamburg and that on the following day the new Royal Air Force Wing in Russia had been in action alongside Soviet air forces near Murmansk. At that time there were two signals relating to the initial operations by 151 Wing of the RAF at Murmansk which were published in the

London and Soviet press. They passed between Air Chief Marshal Portal, Chief of the British Air Staff, and Admiral Kuznetsov, Head of the Soviet Navy and Naval Air Service. Portal wrote:

'British Air Squadrons have arrived in the USSR and are now operating from Soviet territory against the common enemy. On this first and memorable occasion of our two Air Forces fighting side by side on Russian soil I send you the warmest congratulations of all ranks of the Royal Air Force on the skilful and heroic resistance maintained by the Soviet Air Force against the German invaders.

'Permit me to express the confident hope that this may prove the beginning of ever wider and closer collaboration between our two Air Forces, each of which is already straining to the utmost to hasten the final defeat and collapse of the Nazi aggressors.'

Kuznetsov replied: 'I am happy to confirm receipt of your telegram on the occasion of the first RAF operations at MURMANSK. These operations are the very real expression of the inflexible will of the two great freedom-loving peoples who have mobilized their armed and economic might for a decisive and merciless fight against the German invaders.

'I am sincerely happy at the fact that the lucky chance of beginning operations against the common enemy side by side with the RAF on an important part of the Front has fallen to the Air Force of the Soviet Navy.

'I take this opportunity of expressing to you, Air Chief Marshal of the British Royal Air Force, my sincere regards and respect.'

The full text of these exchanges was copied and put up on all notice boards throughout the camp of Vianga. This naturally gave everybody an added sense of unity and purpose. The fact that the first operations of their Wing in Russia had attracted the attention of High Command both in Britain and Russia was for them an extraordinary achievement and made them feel very special and important.

*   *   *

Following their Squadron's four victories on 17 September Wag Haw and Ibby Waud were in particularly good form when they set off to take their bath in the village the following day. That afternoon, shouldering haversacks containing soap and towels, they joined a group of NCOs waiting outside HQ for the arrival of the three-tonner. The Russians had made the baths available for airmen on four afternoons a week and for officers on two evenings. Nobody knew what to expect and they were making jokes about it.

As the truck rumbled up Flight Sergeant Barkus drew himself up and bellowed, 'Steam bath party — fall in. You lucky people!' They bounced along a rough country road for about fifteen or twenty minutes before the truck drew up in front of the brick-built edifice. Jumping off the tailboard of the three-tonner they got their first glimpse of the village at ground level. There were no pavements or other such refinements and the surrounding wooden shacks made the place look like some primitive outpost in the middle of nowhere, which indeed it was.

Having taken off their clothes in the locker room they entered the shower-bath where freezing cold and scalding hot water gushed down from sprays. In the midst of soaping themselves, larking about and indulging in the luxury of having a good scrub up they were astonished to be confronted by a couple of middle-aged Russian women. Dressed in overalls with peasant scarves around their heads and wearing rubber boots the women proceeded to clean up the floors and adjust the water supply and temperature.

The odd sensitive chap covered up his working parts or turned his back to the women feeling decidedly uncomfortable which brought roars of laughter from the others. Most of them were a trifle embarrassed for a moment or two but out of bravado they weren't going to show it. One particular chap, however, was horrified and turned his face to the wall as a woman approached him. She had an amused expression and smacked him smartly on the behind as she went past him and went away shaking with laughter.

In the cloudy atmosphere of the steam room Wag tapped Ibby on the shoulder and pointed to a woman who was operating a small wheel controlling the steam. Her proportions were enormous and Wag in fits of laughter said that she was the largest woman that he had ever seen. Dressed like the others and with similar Mongolian features she stood impassively beside the wall like a giant inflated dummy turning her tiny wheel. Ibby was transfixed watching the beads of perspiration trickling down her flat nose and high cheekbones and he couldn't help himself staring at her vast girth and sheer size. 'My God', he said in his dour Yorkshire way, 'I'd sooner go LMF than make a pass at her!' (Being labelled as 'lacking in moral fibre' was a fate worse than death for any self-respecting fighter pilot.)

Having made several visits to the hot and cold department and when they could no longer endure the steam cooking they finally cooled off and got dressed, feeling totally invigorated and shining clean. After sweating the impurities out of the system for half-an-hour, however, they did notice the cold on the way back in the three-tonner, which until then hadn't bothered them. Ibby had a theory that it was essential to stoke up on the rich, oily Russian diet. 'That's why the Russians eat all that stuff', he said knowingly, 'in order to keep out the cold.' The somewhat debilitating effects of the Turkish style bath soon wore off that evening because apart from the inevitable smoked salmon and other delicacies they had goose on the supper menu. Walking back through the silver birch plantations after a nightly session in the Mess they saw the Northern Lights in all their glory. They shot up like bent searchlights in white and greenish purple flames continually changing their beams and looking for all the world like a gigantic firework display.

The weather was dull on the following day, conforming to the usual pattern of having one good day when the Wing could complete a full operational programme and others when there was little or no flying. Only one patrol went out and saw nothing but an overhanging blanket of grey mist blending in with the tundra landscape. It was like flying low over the English Channel in bad weather with no horizon and being forced to rely on instruments to avoid hitting the sea.

Having to kill time when there was no flying was always a problem for fighter pilots and in Russia it was an exceptionally boring affair. All they could do was to hang about in the Flight hut waiting for something to happen. There was no radio, only the Squadron gramophone with a selection of a dozen records which they knew by heart. Playing cards, chess, draughts, darts and talking amongst themselves helped to pass the time. There were no newspapers or magazines, only books which some had managed to bring with them.

Most pilots preferred to stay in the Flight hut when the weather had closed in and the Squadron had been stood down for the day because there was no bar open and nowhere to go. At least at dispersal they could kick a football around and be close to their aeroplanes! Meals made a break and there was always booze and games in the Mess to while away the evenings. There were opportunities to go into the local cinema in the village but nobody as yet had ventured the seventeen miles into Murmansk for several reasons. Basically transport was in short supply and Russian passes were extremely difficult to acquire. Murmansk was technically in the front line and passes required photographs, signatures and a long delayed and detailed process of registration.

The bad weather continued and apart from the odd air test only two patrols went out on 20 September. The only consolation for the pilots was that they were getting some flying hours in, because there was no sign of the enemy. It was a day when HQ staff were given an airing with plenty of exercise. Wing airmen could be seen all over the camp digging slit trenches and a fire-fighting squad was being organized outside HQ. So far the Luftwaffe hadn't made a concerted attack on the airfield but the Wing was obviously preparing for such an eventuality.

Hubert Griffith, the Wing Adjutant, recorded in his diary that Wing Commander Ramsbottom Isherwood and the two squadron commanders, Tony Rook and Tony Miller had been invited to a rather special party that evening. A neighbouring Russian squadron had been awarded the Order of the Red Banner and had taken over the officers' club house in the village of Vianga to celebrate. Group Captain Bird who was up from the Embassy staff in Moscow and two officer interpreters made up the RAF contingent.

On the following morning Griffith wrote: 'It seems to have been quite a bit of a party last night, with a concert, two suppers (one before the concert, and one at half-time), dancing and endless mixed drinking. The Russians have been at their tricks again, trying to deceive their innocent guests as to the alcoholic potency of vodka. The CO — usually the world's early riser — does not appear at breakfast, neither do the two Squadron Leaders. (They have all no doubt woken, cocked their eye at the weather — the pilot's first instinct on waking — and decided that as it is impossible operationally, they might as well lie in.) Other members were still counted unserviceable after lunch.'

Russian technical officers and their interpreters would often drop into the RAF Mess for meals and a chat with their opposite numbers. They were extremely polite and good natured but found difficulty in referring to English ranks, especially 'Squadron Leader' and 'Flight Lieutenant'. To overcome this problem they addressed the wireless and engineering Flight Lieutenants as 'Meester Feesher' and 'Meester Gittins'. It was quite extraordinary, therefore, that these technical officers were able to discuss highly complex problems with complete understanding on both sides. Gittins had had previous experience on the aerodrome at Keg-Ostrov outside Archangel when he enlisted the help of a Russian engineering officer to make essential assembly tools including aircraft spanners which had been left behind in England. It seemed that in the realms of technology there was some kind of common language which either by signs or mystic means enabled people to communicate and read one another.

★   ★   ★

The first real snow fell on the camp on 22 September and there was quite a snowstorm. A great swirling cloud emptied itself over the surrounding landscape disgorging thick snowflakes whipped by the wind, making it difficult to breathe or see more than a few feet outside. The storm lasted for about ten minutes leaving clear blue sky and then it became heavy again with more snow and rain clouds. Dispersal areas were turned into quagmires and the bumpy sandy surface of the aerodrome became full of puddles, some of which were as large as small lakes. The late autumn weather had arrived producing a cycle of snow, rain and sleet leaving everything indescribably filthy.

Surprisingly the following morning was clear and bright allowing 81 Squadron to escort Russian dive bombers across Finland into Norway. It was a longish trip lasting for well over an hour and the Hurricanes had to fly hard to keep station. The rate of climb and cruising speed of the Russian Pe-2 dive bombers was such that the British escorting fighters were forced to use a lot of throttle to keep pace. Shortly after the Squadron had landed the Russians came on the line saying how pleased they were with the escort job.

Now that the snow had come the weather experts had forecast that good flying days would be limited to little more than six a month as an outside estimate. It appeared that they were going to be proved right because the morning of 25 September was a frothy mixture of light snow, sleet and heavy rain. Leaves were cascading down from the silver birch plantations making the camp look bare and desolate.

The weather cleared up a little in the afternoon although there was no possibility of any operational flying. Despite this the day proved to be a turning point in the activities of 151 Wing. Major General Kuznetsov who was the Russian AOC had been down to the airfield on a number of occasions to get instruction on flying the Hurricane. He was a spare-built man in his late thirties with close greying hair and had a round humorous face and slightly pointed nose. The Wing Adjutant, Flight Lieutenant Griffith, described him as '... one of the most charming personalities I have ever met — very quiet and reserved but with an ever present sense of humour and a way of saying little but to the point. He always did everything he could for us and if he wanted us to do anything he put it to us in such a way that we felt we had suggested it.'

Kuznetsov always came with a girl interpretress who had been a schoolmistress. She had written down all the cockpit drill and had given him an oral and written examination regarding all the details as if he was her school pupil. He was an expert pilot with thousands of hours to his credit and had been a flying instructor so nobody had any doubts that he would have no problems in flying a Hurricane for the first time.

After the filthy morning of the 25th the weather eased off and Kuznetsov climbed into his machine. He had been given his own Hurricane with his personal number and the Red Star painted on the fuselage. Conditions were far from ideal with low cloud and a rough waterlogged airfield as he ran up his Rolls-Royce Merlin engine prior to take off.

Wing Commander Ramsbottom Isherwood, who was watching the proceedings betrayed no sign of anxiety but he must have been mentally 'crossing his fingers' as Kuznetsov taxied out, hoping like hell that he wouldn't prang. In the event the Russian General did a splendid take off and made a couple of perfect landings. In the words of Flight Lieutenant Micky Rook, 'He put her down as light as a gnat's whisker!'

The General's flight opened the door for the Wing to start functioning as an Operational Training Unit. Bomber escorts and patrols were to continue for the time being but the training of Russian pilots and teaching ground staff the technicalities of servicing was to become of paramount importance. Technical co-operation between Wing staff and their Russian counterparts had been progressing but now the objective was to ensure that the Russians could fly and service their Hurricanes independently.

⋆　　⋆　　⋆

Wag and Ibby had spent the morning in the Flight hut playing cards. Nothing serious like bridge but just the easy games requiring little concentration and no headwork. Sometimes they played chess when there was no possible chance of flying and they could get 'stuck in' but although that particular morning was dull and cloudy the forecasters said that it might improve towards mid-afternoon.

During a break in their card playing Ibby, looking rather thoughtful, remarked that he couldn't understand why the Germans hadn't really tried to knock out the airfield. 'They know we're here alright', he said, 'After all, we've shot down seven of the bastards and we've only lost one'. Wag pointed out that the Germans had already experienced two doses of 81 Squadron and perhaps they weren't too keen on having a third. He rubbed his hands together and said that he wished they would come because he couldn't wait to get up there in amongst the bastards. Ibby was aware that coming from most people Wag's remarks would be considered as a bit of a line shoot and frowned upon. But he knew Wag well enough to know that he was perfectly sincere and his emotions were absolutely genuine.

Ibby noticed that Wag's burst of enthusiasm had raised a few eyebrows amongst the rather older Auxiliary fraternity whose attitude was to play it cool. Their reaction annoyed him momentarily perhaps because he and Wag were not officers and he felt that they should have been. Also his friendship with Wag meant a great deal to him. Since they had teamed up on 504 Squadron at Exeter some nine months ago he and Wag had got to know one another pretty well. Perhaps too well, he thought, because he would have hated to see him go down.

After lunch the heavy grey cloud began to break up and 81 Squadron was briefed to escort Soviet bombers whose target was front line troop concentrations in the Petsamo area. Both Wag and Ibby were down for the show in which 'A' Flight would be escorting dive bombers and 'B' Flight the heavy bombers.

Hubert Griffith wrote in his diary that this particular take off was a magnificent sight. First he saw 'A' Flight in formation take off, tearing across the sandy aerodrome and sending up clouds of spray from the puddles and miniature lakes. Then he heard the great roar of the Pe-2 dive bombers as they lifted into the air from their neighbouring strip. They were followed by 'B' Flight and then finally the Pe-2 FT heavy bombers until the sky above Vianga became filled with the thunder of aircraft jinking about, closing up in formation.

The formation climbed hard in an easterly direction towards Petsamo, crossing south of the Kola inlet which gradually narrowed as they gained height. Ten thousand feet below Wag

164

could see the Tuloma River veering south from Kola until it branched out into the Lotta and Notta Rivers making a distinctive 'Y' shape where the water divided. Great bundles of clouds looking like giant bulbous golf balls in grey, dirty brown and purple mantles trundled across the landscape and the formation altered course every now and then to fly through the gaps.

It wasn't long after they had levelled out, flying about a thousand feet above the bombers when black powder puffs of heavy flak burst away to their left. The RT was crackling and Wag was screwing his head round all the time looking out for a glimpse of any Huns in the area but there was no sign of them. Every time they got near clouds the air became turbulent and he had to work hard on the controls feeling his face sweating underneath his oxygen mask. He only realized that the bombers had dropped their loads when the Hurricane ahead of him banked gently and did a wide sweep, finally heading due west back towards Vianga. Looking down he could see the bomber formation and over to his right vanishing powder puffs of flak still hung suspended in the air. He searched around but there was no sign of the dive bombers or the Hurricanes covering them.

A few seconds later he glanced up and behind him and saw an Me 109 hurtling straight down on him. Automatically he pushed the throttle wide open, yanked the stick back and pulled the aircraft into a steep climbing turn. His eyes were everywhere as his machine with its nose to the heavens vibrated in the spiral struggle to gain height. Kicking on the rudder he fell out of the climb and looked round for a bandit he could have a go at.

Way down below he saw a Messerschmitt break away from a circling Hurricane and he dived down on it, feeling his controls getting heavier as his speed built up. In the dive his heart missed a few beats as an Me 109 chased by a Hurricane flashed underneath his nose but he kept on going with his eyes riveted on his bandit.

The 109 saw him and immediately turned towards him, narrowing the angle of attack and both aircraft broke away before they got close as they hurtled towards each other. Using the speed of the dive he pulled out sharply into a climbing turn and pointed his nose towards the German, rapidly overhauling him and closing in on his target from below and beneath. The 109, having temporarily lost sight of him whipped into a turn to find him and in that instant he was able to get the German in his sights and hold him there as he closed range.

Easing his stick back he got the bead of his gunsight ahead of the

109 and fired a long burst narrowing the angle in the turn. By this time he was behind the German and he fired a short burst knowing that he must have clobbered him. The enemy aircraft suddenly puffed out white vapour and then flicked over on to its back before going straight down, leaving a trail of black smoke in the air behind it.

All his concentration had been riveted on that bandit during their duel and in the few seconds that he saw it flick and dive he looked behind and caught a glimpse of another 109 rocketing down on him from behind.

His instant reaction was to yank the Hurricane round and round in a circle and he kept on easing back on the stick and tightening the radius of the turn. His Merlin engine was roaring flat out and his machine juddering on the point of stall but he knew for certain that it could out turn that clipped wing Messerschmitt and there was nothing that the bastard could do about it.

The German zoomed up and down and kept on making stabs at him, coming in like an express train but unable to get his bead on the Hurricane. Wag was bloody glad he had practised the tight turn manoeuvre so many times that he could fly his machine on the verge of stalling without making the fatal mistake of flicking out when the 109 would have got him. The Messerschmitt had buzzed round him like an angry bee until the pilot realized that he wasn't going to be able to nail him and turned away.

In that split second Wag dived and chased him, coming up within range and, having got him in his sights, pressed the firing button. He pressed the button again and again but nothing happened, and he realized that he must have run out of ammunition. The German pilot saw him and turned in on the Hurricane once more. Wag thought that he had had it. His reaction was literally to hurl his machine at the 109 and it veered away to avoid a collision.

Wag immediately half rolled and dived straight for the ground, pulling out right on the deck, having seen the 109 coming after him. He knew that his only chance of survival was to hedge hop his way home without giving the German an opportunity of getting in a burst. The fear of being hunted by a Messerschmitt steadily catching up with him had gone out of his mind as he wrestled with his aircraft. Trees, scrub, rocks, and hillocks had rushed towards his windscreen as he skimmed over the surface of the tundra landscape. He hugged the ground and almost scraped the bottom of one valley in his race for home.

He had no idea when or where the German turned back as he approached the airfield and pulled up into the circuit. Even throttling back and putting his wheels down was an effort. The chase had been like watching a speeded up film going faster and faster as it ran out of control. His mind seemed to clog up as he brought the Hurricane in to land and he had to force himself to concentrate when he touched down.

He taxied into dispersal, revved up his engine, closed the throttle and switched off like a zombie. Pulling off his helmet he sat in his cockpit unable to get out feeling totally limp and completely drained of energy. His mind and reactions to things going on around him had temporarily seized up and it was several minutes before he had the strength to lift himself out. His knees buckled when he jumped off the mainplane and he had to lean against the fuselage for support while trying to stabilize himself.

He saw by the look on the faces of his ground crew that word had got round that the Squadron had been in action. Somewhat wearily he gave them the thumbs-up sign and walked slowly back through the mud and slush towards the steps leading down into the Flight hut. He grabbed his pipe and plonked himself down on a wickerwork chair with his knee trembling as it usually did after some hairy action.

His watch told him that he had been airborne for an hour and he heard the Squadron Commander Tony Rook telling the chaps that Major General Kuznetsov had been on the line personally to thank the Squadron for putting up such a good show. Apparently six Me 109s had jumped 'B' Flight, who had shot down three without loss and all the Russian bombers had returned safely. Wag wondered why those German fighters hadn't gone for the Russian bombers instead of having a go at the British Hurricanes. Perhaps, he thought, the bastards wanted to even up the score which now stood at ten to one in favour of the RAF. It seemed incredible to him that having caught 'B' Flight with its trousers down those 109s hadn't nailed the odd Hurricane on the bounce.

Ibby, who had flown with 'A' Flight which hadn't been involved in the action, sauntered across in his slow deliberate fashion, 'I don't know, Wag', he said with a puzzled grin on his face, 'You are a jammy bastard aren't you?' This remark lifted Wag out of his rather knackered state and he explained to Ibby how a 109 had bloody nearly got him, becoming quite excited in the retelling. 'It's not that bloody funny', he said, 'having no ammo and a 109 up your arse!' At that point Tony Rook came over and patted him on the shoulder, 'Wag', he said, 'you are a jammy bastard!' and then he moved away. It made Ibby's day.

*　　*　　*

Despite the rather gloomy picture painted by the weather pundits who forecast that good flying days would be few and far between, the weather on the 27th was first class. There were a few clouds about but these were high as 81 Squadron took off in the morning to escort Russian bombers. Once again the Squadron was involved in a scrap with Me 109s and shot down two, making the score twelve to one in its favour. The sister squadron No 134 had done a like number of patrols and bomber escort operations but had never come within striking distance of the enemy. It was becoming extremely frustrating for 134 pilots who on the other side of the airfield had spent countless boring hours on 'readiness' only to find that when the action took place 81 Squadron had had all the luck.

This sense of frustration might well have had something to do with a tragic accident which happened at lunchtime that day. The Luftwaffe who had been taking a beating from 151 Wing since its arrival in Russia had sent a Ju 88 on a reconnaisance mission to photograph the airfield at Vianga. This action was undoubtedly in preparation for an air strike and when the German aircraft arrived on the scene 134 Squadron on readiness was immediately scrambled.

The surface around the 134 Squadron dispersal bays was so waterlogged, marshy and sloping that pilots had to use a great deal of engine power to get through it. In order to keep the tail down during this process two airmen were required to drape themselves over the tail end of the fuselage to add extra weight. For them it was a somewhat breezy and mucky business but an essential chore.

In his eagerness to get at the Ju 88 which had appeared overhead Flight Lieutenant Vic Berg opened up his throttle to take off with the airmen still on his tail. The Hurricane gathered speed and when Berg eased back on the stick to lift the aircraft off the ground it went straight up in the air to a height of fifty or sixty feet before falling away and diving into the airfield. The two airmen were killed but Berg, who received very serious leg injuries, survived after being taken to hospital in Murmansk. Both pilot and airmen had been keen and anxious to get the aircraft off the ground and into action as quickly as possible and this misunderstanding was undoubtedly the result of combative zeal. Either the airmen didn't get Berg's signal or he assumed that they had already dropped off. It was a bitter pill for 134 Squadron to swallow but fortunately the only incident of its kind during the Wing's expedition to Russia.

Later that day the Finns who were fighting alongside the Germans broadcast on the radio that they had taken Kandalaksha. This town was about 150 miles south of Murmansk and of great strategic importance. It provided the railway junction linking Murmansk with the Archangel, Leningrad and Moscow network. All supplies of men and materials from these major centres had to go through Kandalaksha on their way up to the Murmansk front. If the Finnish claim proved to be correct then an enemy advance across the railway link would pose serious problems for the Russians and also for the Wing, which would be cut off from rail supplies from Archangel.

During the next day there were conflicting reports about the situation at Kandalaksha. The Russians denied the Finnish claim that it had been taken and British radio announced it as rumour only. This was a Sunday and the weather was exceptionally good for flying. Four bomber escort operations were carried out without any losses or contact with the Luftwaffe. Pilots reported, however, that the flak along the Petsamo front was getting heavier all the time. This was hardly surprising because the Germans were moving up all the heavy artillery they could muster in a desperate attempt to break through before winter set in.

Bridges were prime targets for Russian bombers and on this particular Sunday (28 September) the 100-yard long wooden bridge over the River Petsamojoki was singled out for an attack. This river ran alongside the Arctic Ocean road which provided a vital supplies link running right down from the Rybachiy Peninsula to the Gulf of Bothnia on the Baltic Sea. The bridge was the sole supply line for an entire front held by the 2nd and 3rd Mountain Divisions and therefore an important target. If the bridge could be put out of action for any length of time this would leave the German army on the other side of the river isolated, unrelieved and without sufficient food supplies.

The Germans had ensured that their vital bridge was heavily defended and the Russian bombers encountered heavy and accurate flak on the approach which increased in its intensity as the aircraft dived on it before releasing their 500 lb bombs. Explosions sent up great mushrooms of water and muck and dust from the river banks making it impossible to see whether the bridge itself had been knocked out. Only a later reconnaisance would settle the issue but Russian bomb aimers reported that the attack had been accurate and there was a strong possibility that the bridge had been damaged. About that time Ibby Waud on a bomber escort mission wrote in his log book, '... Saw bridge blown up — some flak!'

The noise of Soviet bombers and anti-aircraft fire had just died away when the entire bank of the river valley began to tremble and shake as if suddenly struck by an earthquake. The stretch of land about 1,500 ft wide between the Petsamojoki River and the Arctic Ocean road became rippled with convulsions and began moving. Slowly millions of cubic yards of earth started slipping and then cascading down on the bridge crushing it as if it had been matchwood. Surrounding troops gazed in horror as they saw entire birch plantations uprooted and pitchforked into the river-bed.

Worse was to follow. The Petsamojoki was a relatively large river and it began to rise up and flood the Arctic Ocean road — the German life-line of the whole Northern Russian front. The landslide brought about by the Russian bombing attack completely obliterated the bridge and changed the surrounding landscape, leaving some 15,000 German troops as well as 7,000 horses and mules totally isolated. Telephone lines disappeared into the river and the flooding of the Arctic Ocean road cut off the supplies route and left thousands of vehicles stranded.

The Germans tried to explain this severe military setback as being the result of some geological fluke saying that the Russians had just been very lucky. There is some substance to this argument but the fact remains that the Russians planned and executed the bombing operation most efficiently. In the havoc and confusion surrounding the bridge immediately after the attack it was impossible for anybody to tell whether the bridge had been seriously damaged because seconds later it disappeared. There is no doubt that the Russian bombing was accurate as bombs set off the landslide around the bridge itself. Natural disaster or not, all units and the headquarters staff of Major General Schnörner's 6th Mountain Division in the neighbouring area had to be diverted to Parkkina to cope with the situation.

To allow flood water to get away the German sappers had to dig vast channels through the mountain of earth and muck which had slipped into the river bed. Then a double footbridge had to be built across the river so that food, fodder, ammunition, fuel and other vital supplies could be manhandled across and then dragged up to the front lines by horses and mules. Whilst this work was progressing other sappers began the awesome task of building a new bridge across the Petsamojoki river.

Way up in the wilderness of the remote Petsamo region the job of spanning that river defies description. Assembling materials was a major problem. Heavy timber had to be obtained from a saw-mill over 120 miles away, lighter planks brought round the coast from Kirkenes in Norway by ship and thousands of lengths of round timber extracted from the timber stores of Petsamo's nickel mines.

All this work took time — which the Germans did not have on their side. Those battalions of the 2nd and 3rd Mountain Divisions who had been in action on the eastern bank of the river since June had to be relieved. According to field reports these men were finished both physically and mentally. Meanwhile the line had to be held at all costs because it was to serve as a springboard for a new and desperate offensive to take Murmansk.

Eleven days after the Russian bombing attack the new bridge was completed and named the 'Prince Eugen Bridge' after Eugen of Savoy in recognition of the Austrian Mountain troops who were the mainstay of General Dietl's Mountain Corps. This was undoubtedly a magnificent achievement in conditions of great hardship and the job was done two days ahead of schedule. At last things could get moving again but fate still held something in store for those German troops on that sector of the front.

On 9 October when everything was set to go, a terrifying Arctic gale raged and howled across the region bringing with it blinding snow and freezing temperatures. All movement was brought to a grinding halt as snowdrifts whipped up by an icy wind buried vehicles which tried to get through. Columns of men who had been carrying supplies got lost in the blizzard and were frozen to death. The icy finger of an approaching Russian winter had negated everything and all the Germans could do for the time being was to go to ground and fight to stay alive.

*　　*　　*

While the Germans had been dealing with their horrendous problems surrounding the Petsamojoki bridge, life in the camp at Vianga carried on as usual. On 28 September when the Russians bombed the bridge two events took place outside the normal routine.

The first concerned little Corporal Flockhart who was marched in to Wing Commander Ramsbottom Isherwood's office to confront the CO on a very serious matter. Flockhart was an assistant carpenter — which was hardly a death or glory occupation, but there was far more to Flockhart than met the eye. Prior to his woodworking activities he had been an air gunner in Whitleys and it was this experience which led to him being up before the CO. The Wing Adjutant recorded that Flockhart 'had drifted off, with no official sanction, and taken part in an operational raid over the Lines as air gunner in a Russian bomber'.

How he managed to achieve this amazing feat was a story in itself. Apparently he had been in the Merchant Navy before the war and during his voyages he had called in at Archangel and made contacts there. When the Wing landed, Flockhart somehow renewed his contacts who gave him introductions to Russian bomber aircrews at Vianga and they arranged it.

Flockhart's unique offence was not catered for in the rule book and King's Regulations did not provide the answer. The Wing Adjutant, knowing that the CO was a strict disciplinarian wondered how he would react. In the event the CO's discourse in the orderly room was, according to the Wing Adjutant, sharp and to the point. He said, in his clipped New Zealand accent: 'Personally, I admire your spirit. Personally, I think it a bloody good show. But all the same, if you had got shot down you'd have put me in the soup, see? Now get out!'

The story soon got round and everybody was astonished, wondering how Flockhart managed to do it — especially with the language barrier. The Russians must have smuggled him out, they thought, because nobody in their right mind would venture out of camp on their own. So Flockhart's exploit became quite an event and like the CO they all thought 'it was a bloody good show'.

The weather was suddenly getting much colder and the CO having talked to his Senior Medical Officer decided that now was a good time to commence the evening issue of rum to airmen of the Wing. This might appear to be a very simple operation but Hugh Griffith said that there had been as much work in organizing the rum ration as in preparing a large scale movement order for the Wing. 'For days past', he said, 'my notebook has been jotted with notes about drawing the rum, diluting the rum, getting exact noggins made to measure out the regulation 1/2-gills of rum, neither more or less, detailing sergeants to supervise the dishing out of the rum, etc, etc,' and he went on to say that, 'the paramount aim of all this supervision is, of course, that no airman shall, by doing a deal with another airman who "don't drink the stuff", be able to get two tots per evening, or alternatively drink his tot neat. The Navy have a traditional method of diluting it and dishing it out. We have to improvise our own arrangements.' Griffith must have done a very good job because none of the 550 airmen got tight and there was no rowdiness.

Wag Haw and Ibby Waud in company with others who had been on board the aircraft carrier *Argus* were experts because they had previously sampled the midday rum ration in Naval style and had found it to be most powerful stuff and very comforting. When asked how he enjoyed the RAF version Wag was non-committal, 'We didn't drink the rum ration every evening', he said quite seriously, 'because gin was only four and sixpence a bottle!'

He was of course, putting on an act because there had been very little drinking amongst the pilots except at the odd party, which happened but rarely. As there was nowhere to go and nothing much to do the Mess was the only retreat at the end of the day. Whiling away a few hours chatting, playing games and having a few drinks became the normal routine.

The last two days of September were uneventful mainly because the weather was duff and only the one bomber escort operation by 134 Squadron described earlier was carried out. The Russian bomber crews and the British fighter pilots hadn't been in close contact in the air — a situation which Ibby Waud attempted to change. When they were heading for home after the Soviet bomber chaps had done their stuff he thought it would be rather fun to close in and show them something of our formation flying.

The Russian bombers flew in rather wide and open formation and Ibby and his chum joined them, flying alongside absolutely wing tip to wing tip. The Soviet pilots responded to the challenge and closed up their own formation and Ibby could see their rear gunners leaning out of their turrets and giving the thumbs-up sign!

The following day the Wing received a signal from the Secretary of State for Air, Sir Archibald Sinclair, which was pinned up on the HQ notice board. It read, 'The destruction by your squadrons of 12 German aircraft for the loss of only one of your own is a brilliant achievement; it is a source of particular pleasure and satisfaction to us here that you are working so closely and so successfully with the Russian Air Force. Good luck to you, 151 Wing.'

Chapter 10
Snow in October

The last day of September and the first in October confirmed the weather men's forecast that good flying days would be few and far between. The sky remained grey and heavy with low, bulbous cloud overhanging the landscape, pregnant with rain, sleet and light snow. A few air tests and some local flights were carried out between outbursts of heavy rain and sleet but there was no operational flying.

During a period of very heavy rain on 3 October the Russians suddenly announced that the camp's water supply would be cut off until five o'clock in the afternoon. This didn't sound too bad and nobody gave it a thought until the announcement was corrected. It emerged that the water supply was actually going to be non-existent for a period of five days which was an entirely different matter. The Russians explained that with the coming of winter they had to lag and bury their mains deep in the ground against the approach of frost.

The Wing Adjutant immediately prepared orders to ration the existing supplies which had been stored. Every airman on the camp would have to make do with a pint of water per day which wasn't much. The officers fared rather better because their batmen were instructed to catch the rain water in buckets as it cascaded down off the Kremlin roof. The Adjutant recorded his sentiments in his diary, 'A return to primitive life with a vengeance! — but on the whole rather fun. By way of contrast — one of the everlasting contrasts that make life here so fascinating — champagne and pancakes for supper!'

No mail from home either official or personal had reached the Wing since it had been formed in England some nine weeks previously and this was causing some discontent amongst the airmen. They knew that several convoys and flying boats had been entering Russia since they left the old country and couldn't understand why these hadn't brought a few bags of mail. Only recently they had read in a Moscow news sheet, printed in English, that Lord Beaverbrook's party were in Moscow and there had been reports of other delegations from Britain which had arrived on special missions. The CO reported the matter to the Air Ministry whose response was that; 'Mail will be despatched in convoy loading in England now...' which was a sure sign that some authority back home had made a 'cock-up' or forgotten about them.

That evening in the Sergeants' Mess Wag heard a rumour that the Russians had come up with the splendid idea of paying 1,000 roubles to any British pilot who had a confirmed victory. If this was good 'gen', he thought, then he and Ibby would have 5,000 roubles between them — it all sounded too good to be true. Neither he nor Ibby had the faintest idea what a rouble was worth in English money but 5,000 of them must represent a fair sum.

The problem, Ibby said, was that even if they got the loot there was nowhere to spend it. There was supposed to be a shop in Vianga but nobody could find it and they didn't know about Murmansk because they hadn't visited the place. Wag considered the situation and concluded that the RAF might give them a credit for the roubles because the RAF wouldn't want to upset the Russians. 'We can have a glorious piss-up when we get home', he said. But Ibby wasn't convinced, 'You know as well as I do, Wag', he replied with a knowing look, 'we'll never get that money. You wait and see.'

Ibby's gloomy prediction came true but not quite as he had imagined. During supper in the Officers' Mess that evening the CO had broached the subject by telling pilots that the usual Russian Air Force tariff of 1,000 roubles per enemy aircraft destroyed would be paid by the Soviet authorities to those Wing pilots who had confirmed victories. This now amounted to 12,000 roubles, he said, which was about £240 at the agreed rates of exchange and he asked them what to do with the money. There were amused cries from the pilots and one called out, 'We can't take it! It would spoil our amateur status!' Eventually, it was agreed that the money given by the Russians should be transferred to the RAF Benevolent Fund in London.

The first official visit to Murmansk was made by a party of twenty or more officers on the following evening in transport laid on by the Russians. For weeks they had been going about in battledress, flying boots, Irvin jackets and, in some cases, wearing fur hats which they had acquired from the Russians — anything and everything to keep them warm and dry. It gave everybody going on the trip a rather strange feeling that life had suddenly returned to normality to find batmen laying out best uniforms and polishing buttons.

While waiting for the transport to arrive one of the more intellectually minded young Pilot Officers began airing his knowledge of Murmansk. 'Do you know', he said, 'Murmansk was built with British capital. I can tell you that the port was full of Allied stores in the First World War like it is today. The Royal Marines were sent up here to defend it from German attacks. Talk about history repeating itself! And the Russians, even in those days, had a four-engined bomber.'

The party endured a long drive over rough roads in the dusk before reaching the outskirts of Murmansk. It was a large straggly place consisting mainly of wooden shacks with a few tall blocks of brick-built flats. The atmosphere was that of a garrison town with but a sprinkling of civilians on the primitive pavements amongst lots of uniforms. The transport pulled up in front of a large and imposing building known as the 'House of Culture' which was obviously the hub of life in the town. The entrance to this vast emporium was a little austere but pleasant with wide stone steps leading up to a paved terrace crowned with a group of bronze statues.

A large area of beautifully laid parquet flooring adorned with a grand piano served as a general foyer and was used for dancing during the intervals of the entertainment. The building complex housed a large theatre, a smaller cinema, club rooms and a library. The interior of the theatre was lined with polished woods giving it a stylish appearance and the whole place was scrupulously clean and well kept up except for the lavatories which were obnoxious in the extreme!

Hubert Griffith wrote after the visit that, '... Murmansk, owing to its short distance behind the Line, ranks as a front line town. Thousands of its regular citizens have been evacuated. Those that remain are almost without exception ordnance clerks, Pioneer Corps, members of Army construction companies or have something or other to do with the armed forces. At least half the women are in uniform — wearing boots, khaki tunics, khaki shirts and breeches with a very workmanlike revolver slung around the waist. They are perfectly willing to be danced with in the intervals of the play on this festive Sunday evening ...' Listening to a record all in Russian and dancing with a girl who had a revolver at hand was a unique experience for the young RAF officers but they enjoyed their evening. Despite the 'loos' and the language barrier it was a relief to get away from camp life.

On the morning after the visit to Murmansk pilots looked up to find that the weather had miraculously changed. It appeared to be a good flying day with high clouds and excellent visibility. The Germans thought likewise, and the Luftwaffe planned a major lightning strike on the airfield at Vianga. A force comprising fourteen Junkers 88 bombers escorted by six Messerschmitt 109E fighters was programmed to blast and shoot up Vianga airfield at mid-afternoon.

The Ju 88 was a fast, formidable and well proven German bomber carrying a bomb load of 5,500 lb. Its armament consisted of six movable machine-guns, one in the nose, four above the fuselage in the rear cockpit and one below in a streamlined 'blister'. Apart from normal bombing duties the machine was extremely effective in a dive bomber role and had been used extensively by the Luftwaffe for bombing London, other inland raids and on anti-shipping strikes.

The Wing headquarters had become well accustomed to air raid routine and when the camp's air raid warnings sounded and Russian ack-ack erupted they all dived into slit trenches outside the Kremlin. Even the noise from anti-aircraft fire couldn't drown the crumps of exploding bombs as the Ju 88s dived on the airfield. The ground heaved around bomb blasts and machine-gun bullets scissored up the earth making tracks of jumping mud as German gunners fired staccato bursts raking the airfield. The noise was deafening as those in slit trenches looked up to see the sky pockmarked with blobs of flak and Hurricanes climbing out of sight to meet the attackers.

After several minutes of ear-splitting crescendo the whines, bangs, crumps and rattle of machine-guns stopped as abruptly as they had started leaving people momentarily in a semi-comatose state. After numbed senses and ringing ears had returned to some degree of normality the first reaction of those in command was to find out about casualties and the extent of the damage.

It soon became apparent to the Wing Adjutant from telephone

calls he received, that considering the size of the raid casualties, in his own words, had been 'almost comically slight'. One flight mechanic had got a chip out of his shin and had been taken to hospital to be X-rayed; another flight mechanic had been clobbered by a clod of earth on the head and had received bruises and scratches; poor old Flight Lieutenant Gittins the overworked engineering officer had been blown clean across his workshop but was otherwise unscathed and one of the trucks had had its windscreen bashed in and a tyre punctured. The Wing had had a miraculous escape — but not so the Luftwaffe.

Son ` Hurricanes had been airborne when the attack started and others on readiness were scrambled. In fact, all pilots at dispersals jumped into machines to get off the ground fast. Wag Haw was one of them. He had had a day off and went back to the Flight hut after lunch because there was nothing else to do. The attack happened in seconds and deciding that it was much safer upstairs than down he ran to his machine and managed to take off. Another pilot, Scotty Edmiston, wasn't so fortunate. He was about to get airborne when a bomb dropped in front of his machine stopping his engine. He then climbed out of his cockpit on to the wing and was promptly blown off by another bomb. However, he landed flat into a soft muddy miniature lake which cushioned the impact leaving him intact, a little befuddled but otherwise uninjured.

The day belonged to 134 Squadron because Squadron Leader Tony Miller and his boys broke their previous run of bad luck by shooting down two Ju 88s and also getting three 'probables' and six damaged. It was a terrific performance by 134 who naturally were thrilled to bits, as was the entire camp.

81 Squadron didn't return empty handed because Micky Rook blew an Me 109 to bits. This tall, good-looking Flight commander who personified the Auxiliary attitude had lost contact with his Squadron and had tried to join formation with six Me 109s whom he took absent mindedly to be 134 Squadron Hurricanes. He even waggled his wings as a sign of greeting and comradeship. When he realized his mistake one of the 109s had turned into him and came straight at him, so he gave it a squirt with his twelve guns and blew it out of the sky. Micky admitted afterwards that, 'The Germans must have thought me either bloody brave or bloody foolish.'

But that wasn't quite the end of the story because, to put it mildly, Micky had been to hell and back before he landed. After he had shot down his 109 the remaining five fastened on his tail and chased him down to ground level where he had a real battle for survival for several minutes. He remembered finally flashing past a destroyer lying in Murmansk Sound at mast level before he eventually managed to shake them off. 'When I finally got back to the aerodrome and landed', he said, 'I sat actually sweating in the cockpit for some time before I could climb out.' 'It was bloody dangerous, you know,' he added!

*　　*　　*

Two days later, on 9 October, an Arctic blizzard struck the aerodrome, covering the landscape with thick, heavy snow and whipping it up into drifts in freezing temperatures. This was the weather that had prevented General Dietl's troops from crossing their new bridge over the Petsamojoki River to relieve the German army isolated on the far bank. The men of 151 Wing may have found their first taste of a Russian winter to be most uncomfortable but it came at a most opportune time as far the Northern Russian front was concerned.

The bombing of the Petsamojoki bridge, shortage of supplies and the early arrival of an Arctic winter had combined to stifle the German drive to take Murmansk, which had become a desperate issue. When Hitler had been discussing his invasion plans for this North Russian front with General Dietl he had looked upon the capture of Murmansk as necessary merely to eliminate the Russian threat to the vital ore mines of Petsamo and the Arctic Ocean road.

The Germans now had to contend with the arrival of Anglo/American aid on an ever increasing scale and the capture of the ice-free port of Murmansk with its strategic railway line was a vital issue which might well affect the outcome of the war. It is quite extraordinary that German Intelligence hadn't taken this into account during the planning stages of the campaign because Murmansk had been the haven for Allied supplies during the First World War and history was now repeating itself.

The Red Army on the central front had been retreating and during the first nine days of October German forces had got to within 140 miles of Moscow. This might have encouraged the German High Command to think that it could polish off the Russians fairly quickly and there was time enough to sort out the situation in the Murmansk area. It was in this climate of uncertainty and grave anxiety as to whether Russia might collapse that Britain and America pledged a vast aid programme in which the ports of Murmansk and Archangel were paramount.

Right *Ibby Waud as senior Flight commander of 83 Squadron, after his Russian experience, when he was posted to the Middle East.*

Below *Wag Haw wearing his unique combination of awards: the DFM and the Order of Lenin.*

Above *Squadron Leader Haw explains the intricacies of the office to enthusiastic youngsters, back in Britain.*

*The Order of Lenin **left** and a register **right** which indicates the unusual nature of the awards to members of the Wing when compared with the lesser decorations given to other individuals of considerably higher rank.*

Overleaf *Wag Haw's citation from Vice Admiral Golovko.*

REGISTER

British citizens decorated in the years of The Great Patriotic War
with Soviet Orders and Medals.

ORDER OF VICTORY
1. Field-Marshal Sir B. L. Montgomery. (by decree 5-6-45).

ORDER OF LENIN
1. Wing Commander 29116 H. N. G. Ramsbottom-Isherwood. D.F.C. A.F.C. (27-11-41).
2. Squadron Leader 90071 A. H. Rook. D.F.C. (27-11-41).
3. Squadron Leader 90088 A. G. Miller. D.F.C. (27-11-41).
4. Flight Sergeant 745249 C. Haw, D.F.M., R.A.F.V.R. (27-11-41) .

ORDER OF SUVOROV 1st class
1. Admiral Sir John C. Tovey, (19-2-44).
2. General Sir Harold Alexander, (19-2-44).
3. Air Chief Marshal Sir Arthur Harris, (19-2-44).
4. Admiral Sir Bruce A. Fraser, (19-2-44).
5. Chief of the Imperial General Staff Sir Alan F. Brooke. (26-2-44).
6. Lord Privy Seal, Lord Beaverbrook. (4-10-44).
7. Minister of Production, Oliver Lyttelton, D.S.O. M.C. M.P. (4-10-44).
8. Field-Marshal Sir B. L. Montgomery, (4-10-44).

ORDER OF SUVOROV 3rd class
1. Vice-Admiral Sir R. L. Burnett, (21-3-44).
2. Brigadier 141238 A. D. Ward. The King's Regt. (21-3-44).
3. Air Vice-Marshal W. F. Dickson. (21-3-44).
4. Colonel 14311 R. E. Wood. Royal Engineers (23-5-44).
5. Brigadier 95359 A. H. Earley. Royal Engineers (23-5-44).

ORDER OF KUTUZOV 1st class
1. Air Chief Marshal Sir Trafford Leigh-Mallory. (4-10-44).

ORDER OF KUTUZOV 2nd class
1. Lieutenant-General 12914 Sir A. F. Smith. Coldstream Guards. (23-5-44).
2. Major-General 47947 A. R. Selby. Royal Ulster Rifles. (23-5-44).
3. Brigadier General 1330 A. S. G. Douglas. The Rifle Brigade. (23-5-44).
4. Brigadier General 27513 A. C. F. Jackson. The Hampshire Regt. (23-5-44).

ORDER OF KUTUZOV 3rd class
1. Commodore R. A. Melhuish, R.I.N.R. (21-3-44).
2. Brigadier 195624 F. H. R. MacLean. M.P. Cameron Highlanders(21-3-44).
3. Air Vice-Marshal F. L. Hopps. (21-3-44).

ORDER OF ALEXANDER NEVESKY
1. Captain J. H. F. Crombie, D.S.O., R.N. (21-3-44).
2. Lieutenant-Colonel 5957 W. R. B. Williams. 7th Gurkha Rifles, (21-3-44).
3. Air Vice-Marshal D. C. T. Bennett. (21-3-44).

ORDER OF USHAKOV 1st class
1. Admiral Sir Bertram H. Ramsay. (4-10-44).

ORDER OF THE RED BANNER
1. Commander M. Richmond, O.B.E., R.N. (7-9-42).
2. Commander R. G. Onslow, D.S.O., R.N. (7-9-42).
3. Commander E. P. Hinton, M.V.O. D.S.O., R.N. (7-9-42).
4. Captain J. Lawrie, D.S.O. D.S.C., Master M.N. S.S. Trehata (7-9-42).

C.C.C.P. = THE UNION OF THE SOVIET SOCIALIST REPUBLICS .
H.K.B.M.ΦΡ. = THE COMMITTEE OF THE 'MILITARY' - NAVAL FLEET.

——— · ———

THE COMMANDER
OF THE NORTHERN FLEET

29 NOVEMBER 1941   POLYARNOYE.

TO/ PILOT OF THE ROYAL
'MILITARY' AIR FLEET OF GREAT BRITAIN.

SERGEANT HAW C.F.

I CONGRATULATE YOU WITH THE HIGH GOVERNMENT
AWARD OF THE UNION OF SOCIALIST REPUBLICS ———
— THE "ORDER OF LENIN".

YOUR MANLINESS, HEROISM AND EXCELLENT MASTERY
IN BATTLES OF THE AIR, HAVE ALWAYS ASSURED VICTORY
OVER THE ENEMY.

I WISH YOU NEW VICTORIES IN BATTLES AGAINST
THE COMMON ENEMY OF ALL PROGRESSIVE NATIONS i.e. —
— GERMAN FASCISM .

VICE-ADMIRAL (SIGNED) A. GOLOVKO

——— · ———

NOTE BY TRANSLATOR: — THE WORD 'MILITARY' IN RUSSIAN
CONVEYS THE MEANING OF
'FIGHTING FORCES' — IRRESPECTIVE
WHETHER ARMY — NAVY OR AIR FORCE.

The shopping list covered Russian Naval, Army and Air Force requirements and was of staggering proportions. For the Navy there were eight destroyers, 3,000 anti-aircraft machine-guns, 1,500 naval guns and 150 'Asdic' submarine detection sets. Monthly deliveries to the Red Army included 1,000 tanks, 300 anti-aircraft guns, 300 anti-tank guns and 2,000 armoured cars. The Red Air Force was to receive 1,800 Hurricanes and Spitfires, 900 American fighters and 900 American bombers in nine-monthly deliveries. These were only immediate requirements and were to be provided with a full back-up of accessories and spare parts.

Anglo-American missions which had gone to Moscow had offered 20,000 tons a month of petroleum products including lubricating oil for aero engines, shipping to transport half-a-million tons of food, oil and war materials per month and vast quantities of medical supplies including ten million surgical needles and half-a-million pairs of surgical gloves. The British and American governments also promised to supply aluminium, copper, tin, brass, nickel, cobalt, steel, industrial diamonds, machine tools, rubber, wool, jute and lead in substantial quantities on a monthly basis.

Prime Minister Winston Churchill was worried at this time about the speed with which aid to Russia could be delivered and put pressure on the Chiefs of Staff Committee to ensure that convoys sailed immediately. A few days later he telegraphed Premier Stalin saying, 'We intend to run a continuous cycle of convoys leaving every ten days.' The Chiefs of Staff had undoubtedly taken his words to heart because shortly afterwards Churchill was able to assure Stalin that convoys would be arriving at Archangel on October 12 and 29 and a third convoy would leave Britain on the 22nd — all laden with consignments of fighters, Bren carriers, guns and ammunition.

During those October days German troops got within 65 miles of Moscow and the British Prime Minister studied the progress of the Russian aid programme every day to ensure that everything humanly possible was being done to help repulse them. But there was one particular area of this complex operation which he singled out as being insufficient and he wrote to Air Chief Marshal Portal saying, '...The most serious mistake we have made about the Russians was in not sending eight Air Force Fighter Squadrons, which would have gained great fame, destroyed many German aircraft, and given immense encouragement all along the front.'

Chapter 11
Phase Two

By the second week in October the Russian winter had laid its permanent mantle of thick, deep, crisp and crackly snow over the landscape and temperatures had gone down to 10-15 degrees Fahrenheit below freezing. The silver birch plantations were bare and the austere airmens' barrack blocks could be seen for the first time from the Wing Headquarters' building about a half a mile away. Horse drawn sleighs began to take over from motor vehicles and out in the open in the clear dry cold atmosphere everything was a dazzling, incandescent white which made one's eyes smart and weep.

The airfield which had become covered with mounds of snow looked like a ghostly lunar landscape until Russian labour forces came out with heavy rollers and flattened it into a congealed mass of frozen snow and sand. They came at night and as they drove past the barracks Wag and Ibby heard their deep voices singing solemn Russian songs in a dramatic chorus, making their hair stand on end!

The time had now come for the Wing to concentrate on its major function, that of training Russian pilots to fly Hurricanes and Russian ground crews to service them. Most of the pilot training was done by 134 Squadron and this began when a Russian officer walked into the 'operations room' and was introduced to Squadron Leader Tony Miller who commanded 134. Tony recalled that meeting and the subsequent events:

'Kapitan Raputsokov was a thickset, cobby sort of chap with a quiet sense of humour. He obviously had a lot of flying experience because his job was to fly round to various units checking out all types of aircraft. Raputsokov told me that he had flown Hurricanes, and by the universally understood gesture of "thumbs-up" indicated that he thought them *'horosho'* — the goods!

'That evening we were entertained by the Russian airmen at the first of the many convivial parties staged between us — and believe me it was some party! Raputsokov sat next to me solid as a rock upon whom waves of alcohol were breaking without any effect whatsoever. Later that evening when Bacchus took over he quietly and politely escorted me through concert halls and dining rooms guiding my wavering footsteps and until I was firmly ensconced in the transit van taking us back to base.

'In the circumstances, and especially as he was a very good type, I decided to make him an honorary member of the Squadron — a rare distinction! Major General Kuznetsov agreed right away when I asked whether Raputsokov could be semi-officially attached to 134 Squadron saying that Raputsokov was going to be the first instructor on Hurricanes anyway.'

That was how 134 Squadron came to do most of the Russian pilot training but unfortunately, Raputsokov never flew with the Squadron in action. He was killed a few days later trying to bring back a crippled Russian bomber which had been clobbered by flak over enemy lines. The bomber crashed near Vianga and he and all the crew were killed.

Russian pilots were only too eager and keen to 'have a go' in the Hurricane. For them it was like stepping into a new streamlined, highly powered and supercharged sports car after their I-16s. This Russian fighter was a stocky, radial engine machine which, although not particularly fast, was very effective in the hands of an experienced pilot. Its manoeuvrability was quite extraordinary but it had a high landing speed and other peculiarities which made it dangerous to novices. One only had to look at its stubby wings and short fuselage to know that it would have some vicious tricks up its sleeves especially when under pressure.

But the I-16, or the 'Rata' as it was named, was a very tough machine with a strong undercarriage and flaps which made it an ideal aircraft for operating out of rough airfields. The Hurricane, by comparison, looked a ladylike and dainty creature. When Russian pilots showed our chaps over their machine they had been keen to point out that it was a difficult aircraft to fly and that 'only the very best pilots could fly it.' The RAF reacted in typical manner saying that Hurricanes were practically viceless and that any Charlie could fly them. 'Nothing to it old boy — it's a piece of cake!' was the general impression given by the British fraternity. In doing their conversion course some of the Russians inevitably made heavy landings damaging wing tips and undercarriages and their British counterparts watching closely would chant in chorus, 'Only the best pilots can fly the I-16. Only the best pilots can fly the I-16.'

The Russian pilots who were older than their British counterparts had many more flying hours to their credit and initially adopted a rather 'know it all' attitude. This attitude changed after they had experienced a few 'prangs' and then they began to take more notice of what the RAF had to say on the subject of handling a Hurricane.

Even Kapitan Safonov, the ace fighter pilot of the 72nd Regiment, managed to damage his flaps after landing, which was probably a good thing because everybody sat up and took notice after that mishap. Actually, Safonov was plumb unlucky in that he ploughed through a miniature lake on the waterlogged airfield after touchdown. But Major General Kuznetsov was not too pleased and it made Safonov more inclined to listen to advice.

Boris Froktistorich Safonov was a fine pilot and a brilliant shot with some twenty confirmed victories to his credit. He had already been awarded the Soviet Order of the 'Red Banner' and later was to receive the highest decoration of all when he became a 'Hero of the Soviet Union'. A large, solid and serious man he was methodical in his approach to flying and a little slow to learn. When he took off in a Hurricane for the first time, for example, he had meticulously prepared everything and made a good straight take-off climbing up to 1,500 ft before attempting to turn and he did three ultra careful circuits and landings with his undercarriage down before doing anything else.

Safonov headed up the training programme on the Russian side and was assisted by a Kapitan Kuharienko who was a short, wiry little man with a permanent grin. The two men were entirely different in character and in their approach to flying. Kuharienko's first trip in the Hurricane was a 'hair raising' performance for everybody except himself. He had jumped into his cockpit and roared away with the rudder trim in the wrong direction. Consequently his take-off was a series of sickening swerves until he finally staggered into the air. Then he decided to demonstrate the aerobatic qualities of the machine by doing a series of flick rolls and generally beating up the airfield. Taxying in to dispersal he had a great beam on his face and after switching off he pointed to the rudder trim control and then tapped his forehead in fits of laughter shouting '*Plocha — plocha*' ('Bad — bad'), regarding the whole thing as a tremendous joke.

Most of the instructing from the English side was carried out by Flight Lieutenant Ross DFC, of 134 Squadron who formed a close association with Kuharienko. 'They are great friends,' Safonov explained, 'because they are both practically dwarfs, and have the same problems in not 'being able to see out of the cockpit.' The Russians couldn't have had a better chap than Ross to explain the Hurricane to them. Hubert Griffith described him in his diary as one of the 'most unfailingly amusing of all our pilots who ever trod Soviet soil.'

Ross, Safonov and Kuharienko formed the team who sent off the Russian pilots for their first solos in a Hurricane and naturally had their problems. Russian pilots were loath to retract their undercarriages which was part of the drill during routine circuits and landings. Neither would they close their hoods because they had been used to open cockpits. The subject was quietly and gently mentioned to Major General Kuznetsov one evening who immediately issued an order stating that any pilot not following instructions on these matters would be grounded indefinitely! As Ross said, 'Thereafter they used to take off, fly, land and taxi with their hoods firmly shut and were so keen to get their undercarriages up the instant they left the ground that we sometimes feared that there would be a premature flop...'

The performance of the twelve-gun Hurricane in Russia made it a lethal fighter in the hands of RAF pilots who had set a high standard for their Russian counterparts to emulate. There had only been a limited number of days during which a full operational programme could be carried out but during that limited period the Wing had shot down fifteen German aircraft for the loss of one Hurricane and damaged or destroyed many others. Furthermore, not one Russian bomber escorted by British fighters had been lost to date.

This achievement did much to engender the respect and even admiration of the Russian hosts who became mad keen to fly the machines. At first they had been inclined to be a little distrustful of the RAF set-up but rapidly thawed out when they had seen for themselves how the Hurricanes performed. They would suddenly arrive and demand training even in the most appalling weather conditions. Squadron Leader Tony Miller remembered one pilot doing his first solo in a snowstorm which he said, 'would have shaken any of us. It took him three shots to get down and each time he went round again and disappeared clean out of sight. I never expected to see him again; however, he managed to get down somehow.'

The darts boards in the Flight huts intrigued the Russians and they became interested and then very keen on the game. Their initial impression that British fighter pilots played darts to improve their aim in air combat was enough to get them going and they played the game with great enthusiasm. So much so that it frequently took a pair of pliers to extract their darts which they hurled like harpoons and practically buried in the darts board.

They did everything with great vigour especially when testing their machine-guns. The normal British method was to fire off a quick burst when airborne but not so the Russians! Getting into the cockpit and pressing the gun button while the aircraft stood in its dispersal bay was far simpler. The fact that several hundred rounds of ammunition sailed over the surrounding hillocks was of no consequence. Perhaps it was the very act of firing off rounds whenever they got into their aircraft which gave them pleasure but eventually they were only persuaded to cease the practice on the grounds that it blew off the gun patches and necessitated constant cleaning of the gun barrels!

Their natural tendency to push anything to the utmost limit of its capabilities had some rather unfortunate results. The word 'maximum' immediately registered in their minds as being an immediate objective. When reading that the Hurricane had a maximum range of 750 miles, for example, one particular pilot saw no reason why he shouldn't be able to cover that distance and proceeded to attempt to do so at full throttle with the inevitable result that he ran out of juice and wrote off his aeroplane. He didn't understand that to go that far he would have to fly at normal operating speed or economical cruising. It took more than the Wing experts could explain and more than one write-off by Russian pilots to teach them the trade off between speed and endurance, particularly under combat conditions.

Similarly with the radio equipment installed in the Hurricane. Russian technicians having been instructed by the wireless officer, Flight Lieutenant Fisher, would take a set away and then attempt to modify it. A couple of days later they would reappear saying,

'Meester Feesher, why won't this wireless set work? What is wrong with it?' In a sense, Russian pilots and technicians were like boys given a new toy and wanting to play with it and take it to bits to see how it worked. The language barrier made things difficult and misunderstandings were bound to arise but in the end the sheer practical experience of the RAF plus a very definite word or two from the General put matters right.

While this technical collaboration was proceeding Flight Sergeant Micky Turner, an ex-Halton apprentice, was selected to go down to the Russian headquarters in the village to help the female translators with the instructions on the maintenance of the Hawker Hurricane. At the time he hadn't understood why he had been chosen because he he said that his Russian was no better than the average 'Joe' but he soon cottoned on to what was required.

Each morning at 8.00 am a Russian driver with a car turned up to take him down to Vianga and the journeys became some of the most terrifying he had ever experienced. 'There was bags of snow', he said, 'and it was obvious that the driver wanted to impress me. He certainly did! We spent much of the time slithering down hills backwards or sideways and spinning off corners, but there was no other traffic. Thank goodness!'

Part of Micky's job was to differentiate to an interpreter a hole, a tube, a bore, a cylinder, a duct, a pipe and other words having a similar meaning. 'It was a great experience for me,' he said, 'because I had a closer association with the Russians than most and lunchtimes always turned out to be an honourable occasion with all the traditional foods they had in their Officers' Mess.'

Micky Turner's Flight commander was the diminutive Flight Lieutenant Ross and one day when he went into the Flight hut to have a word with him he found the pilots jigging about like lunatics. Ross told him that this was all due to the Russian pilot Yacobenko who had made quite an impact on the Squadron. Yacobenko was an ex-cavalry officer whose reason for joining the Air Force was simply that he got bored riding one 'horse' when he discovered that he could harness the power of several hundred of them all at once in the cockpit of a fighter aircraft! One particular morning, when the weather was 'harry clampers' and there was no chance of flying, Tony Miller and two or three others had gone down to visit Yacobenko's squadron. Tony Miller:

'His favourite gesture after muttering "Fascist crafts!" (Fascist aircraft) with extraordinary venom was to mime spitting on the ground, grind in the supposed expectoration with his heel, draw his finger across his throat in ferocious pantomime and then dance and stamp on the floor until the rafters rang and the whole building shook'. This pantomime was immediately adopted by 134 and became their Squadron war dance — which they were practising when Micky Turner walked in.

*　　*　　*

It came as a surprise and a disappointment to the Wing in mid-October to receive a signal from Air Ministry intimating that it might be transferred to the Middle East. After completing the job in Russia most people had assumed that they would be going home. But signals continued to arrive hinting that the Wing would be moving south without being specific about the actual location. When the CO, Wing Commander Ramsbottom Isherwood, had a word with his Russian colleagues about travelling to the Middle East they told him that the journey might take a minimum of two months and probably four or more as they would have to travel via Central and Southern Russia.

The prospect of having to go by rail for some 2,000 miles down through the guts of the huge country was an alarming thought — even the rail journey from Archangel to Murmansk had been a fairly hairy experience! Most people thought that it was a bloody miracle that the overstrained rail network was still able to feed the 2,000-mile front line with military supplies from all over the vast country. Nobody cared to assess what chances the Wing might have of being able to cut across such a network, particularly in view of the current military situation.

Confidence in the project wasn't exactly stimulated when a signal was received from Air Ministry saying that, 'The Embassy and whole of the Military and Air Mission was leaving Moscow that night for Kuibishev.' As the degree of priority on the message was that of 'emergency' it looked as if there was some monumental flap going on. The Wing Adjutant discovered that 'Kuibishev' was the new name for the ancient town of Samara situated about 500 miles to the east of Moscow. The inevitable conclusion was that if embassies were being evacuated in such a hurry then there was a grave danger of Moscow itself being taken by the enemy.

With the rapid German advance into the central section of the front it began to look as if the Wing would have no chance of moving south by rail as the line would be overrun. It was impossible for those in authority back home to contemplate or understand what conditions of railway transport over long distances through the Soviet heartland were like. The Wing Adjutant had already worked out that even if the rail journey was possible the Wing would require at least forty tons of rations for a trip lasting four months or more. Meanwhile all they could do was to carry on with the training programme and hope for the best — hoping that if all else failed the Navy would get them out.

Although the weather had virtually closed in as far as operational flying was concerned the Luftwaffe made a minor strike on the camp on 16 October dropping a few bombs without causing any damage or casualties. On the following day three patrols were carried out without making contact with the enemy and two days later all the Wing's Hurricanes and equipment including even the pilots' flying helmets, Mae Wests and dinghies were handed over to the Russians. After six weeks in action the Wing had ceased to be operational and a signal was sent to Air Ministry on 20 October saying, 'All aircraft handed over to Soviet pilots.'

About this time the Wing Adjutant wrote in his diary that three squadrons of Russian pilots could fly Hurricanes and were expert enough to teach others and Soviet ground staffs were competent at servicing and maintaining them. 'The Wing had carried out', he said, 'the function for which it was originally created — to arrive, to get cracking, to assist others to get cracking on its own type of aircraft, and then to depart.'

There was still some further training to be carried out but the problem facing Wing Commander Ramsbottom Isherwood and his staff was how to keep people occupied when they had little to do. The weather was steadily getting colder and by late October the ink began to freeze in the ink-wells and hours of daylight were diminishing as the Russian winter set in.

'B' Flight of 81 Squadron had handed over their Hurricanes to the Russians some two weeks previously and Wag Haw and his associates had enthusiastically taken up winter sports. Skis had been obtained from the cultural hall in Vianga and the airmen had made up toboggans from packing cases. This cultural centre, combining a cinema and rooms for dancing and political activities, was more primitive and on a much smaller scale than the one in Murmansk where the officers had been entertained. The skis were free and available to the public at large as part of the Russian system of community services.

The pilots soon invented a new and more adventurous kind of winter sport by harnessing the power of a Ford V8 wooden-backed shooting brake to a sleigh which was towed behind at a rope's length. Going at full speed the Ford V8 tended to skid and swerve on the snow hurling the sleigh riders through the air for considerable distances. A brake on this particular and novel sport was officially applied after one Sergeant Pilot had cracked open his skull and others suffered cuts and abrasions.

At this time Ramsbottom Isherwood decided that all the pilots excluding the Squadron commanders should embark on a route march for fitness and issued an order to that effect. He had put this idea into practice when the Wing had time on its hands while assembling at Leconfield before embarking for Russia. It hadn't exactly been well received in England and the prospect of slipping and sliding through the silver birch plantations for a couple of hours during a Russian winter brought forth a storm of protest. But the CO appeared unconcerned and off they had to go, led by the indomitable and good natured Micky Rook of 81 Squadron.

Whenever the weather allowed, a timetable incorporating route marches, rifle shooting, football matches and physical training was put into effect to keep everybody as fit and occupied as possible. But gradually these sports had to be curtailed and finally abandoned as temperatures dropped as low as 5 degrees Farenheit, giving 27 degrees of frost and making the surface like a skating rink. The final fling as far as outdoor sports were concerned was a physical training programme for all young officers commencing at 8.30 am before breakfast. Hubert Griffith wrote that this was started as something of a gesture of defiance to the elements. As he said, PT before breakfast within the Arctic Circle in the month of November would read very heroically in all Squadron record books in after years. When the wind really started blowing, however, they had to stop because of the wind chill factor.

Chapter 12
Arctic winter

The Arctic winter had by now begun in earnest as days contracted into hours of twilight and roads and tracks covered with several inches of snow became packed down hard where traffic and people moved. A Stygian gloom had descended across the landscape allowing only a brief period of proper daylight before and after midday. The Gulf Stream had kept the Barents Sea around Murmansk free of ice and so the port was fast becoming the only haven for the cycle of Russian aid convoys leaving Britain.

The Russians had undertaken to maintain a passage through the White Sea for the whole winter so that British convoys could use the port of Archangel but they were fighting a losing battle. The winter of 1941 had arrived earlier than usual and was much more severe. In a desperate attempt to keep Archangel open the Russians had been using an icebreaker around the clock to cut a channel through the ice on the River Dvina leading into the harbour. But the White Sea — the gateway from the port into the open Barents Sea — was a mass of thickening ice.

It took six weeks for one British convoy 'PQ-4', aided by two icebreakers, to cut through 150 miles of ice in the White Sea in order to get into open water and thereafter the project was abandoned. This left Murmansk as the only open port with access to the Atlantic Ocean for a period of six months until June 1942 when nature would clear the way for ships to use Archangel.

Although fierce fighting was still going on fifty or sixty miles west of Moscow and south in the Ukraine the German advance along the North Russian front had ground to a halt. The Arctic winter hit the Murmansk and Petsamo area eight weeks before it also paralysed German divisions facing Moscow. All that the Germans could do on the Murmansk front was to dig in and try desperately to hold the line until spring came along when they could again begin offensive operations.

Until sub-zero temperatures and blinding snowstorms had confined all military operations to a few patrols the Siberians had maintained a series of suicidal attacks on German positions at the neck of the Rybachiy Peninsula facing Murmansk. This close quarter combat using grenades, rifles and bayonets amongst the rocks and caves of the tundra had prevented the enemy from advancing down the road to Murmansk itself. On the night of 6/7 November on the icy front before Murmansk a German Corporal in a strongpoint thought he heard strange sounds and put his hand to his ear. An easterly wind was blowing and carrying with it obvious sounds of a party with singing and revelry. He distinctly recognized the song of the 'Internationale' and knew that the Russians were up to something so he reported the incident to his company. The Germans knew from experience that whenever the Russians got their hands on vodka bottles anything might happen but they were unsure whether this was simply a celebration or a booze-up before an attack.

The Corporal and his men waited in their strongpoint listening to the Russians making merry and at 4.00 am they heard the cries of *'Urra'* as a Siberian regiment charged their outpost throwing grenades and coming at them with rifle butts, trenching tools and bayonets.

The Russians in the front line had been celebrating the anniversary of the 1917 Revolution which had given them their present government and constitution. These 'November Celebrations' had become a traditional event right across the Soviet Union and hence the supplies of vodka and the party spirit in the wilderness of the tundra country which encouraged the Siberians to charge the German line.

A few miles to the west of the German line of defence another party had been in progress that night in the little village of Vianga. Major General Kuznetsov had invited certain officers of 151 Wing to a formal dinner party also to celebrate the anniversary of the Russian Revolution. RAF Squadron commanders and senior officers mingled with recently decorated Russian officers and lady interpreters in 'afternoon frocks' as Griffith described them.

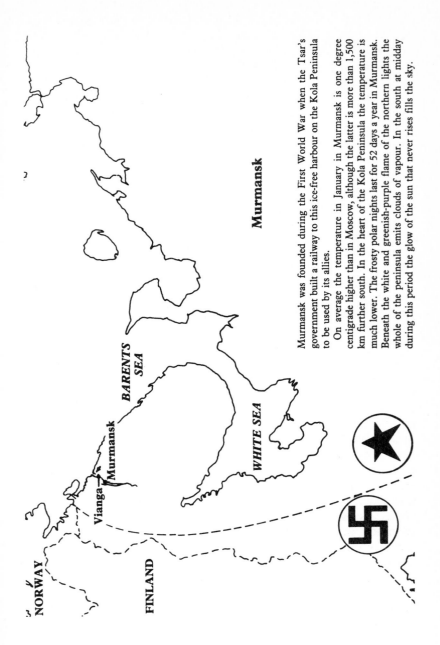

Murmansk

Murmansk was founded during the First World War when the Tsar's government built a railway to this ice-free harbour on the Kola Peninsula to be used by its allies.

On average the temperature in January in Murmansk is one degree centigrade higher than in Moscow, although the latter is more than 1,500 km further south. In the heart of the Kola Peninsula the temperature is much lower. The frosty polar nights last for 52 days a year in Murmansk. Beneath the white and greenish-purple flame of the northern lights the whole of the peninsula emits clouds of vapour. In the south at midday during this period the glow of the sun that never rises fills the sky.

Then the gathering, as was customary, made for the Vianga village hall for speeches and a theatrical performance to be followed by dancing. The place was already crowded with soldiers and local inhabitants when the General's party arrived and everybody was in good form because of the 'Party celebrations'. It came as a surprise to most of the RAF officers in the midst of all the gaiety and fun that the speeches should suddenly concentrate on the gravity of the war situation; figures of Russian casualties were announced reaching a total of two million in November 1941; the position of battle lines and strategy were discussed in accurate detail and the fact that Russia had her back to the wall and was fighting for survival was recognized and not glossed over.

These bitter pills were swallowed by the audience without any outward effect and then the dancing, the singing, the theatrical sketches and the juggling turns proceeded much to everybody's delight. Hubert Griffith recorded in his diary, '...This was at a time, remember, when the Russian advance had not yet begun and was in effect the most critical time of the retreat. And yet, one had the impression, at that time and at that time exactly, that if any member of the Russian audience had got up and suggested the possibility of ultimate Russian defeat, he would not have been put up against a wall and shot as a traitor — but would merely have been laughed at as a polite lunatic...'

During that awful November snow lay several feet deep and icy blizzards raged across the tundra so that even patrols could pass within a few feet of one another without recognition. For German troops it was a question of fighting to stay alive. They cut down telegraph poles linking the Russian lines to Murmansk and burnt them in primitive stoves. Siberian troops retaliated by appearing, like ghosts, out of the gloom and attacking sentries and supply columns. But apart from those forays it was a period of hibernation during which Murmansk and 151 Wing lived a cocoon-like existence.

Life on the camp at Vianga had become a frustrating and idle affair for the young pilots who had literally nothing to do. Meal times and drinks in the Mess in the evening after supper became 'occasions' between hours of gloomy twilight and blackness. The Mess became the retreat and booze was cheap so it was hardly surprising that a good deal of ragging and high spirited fun took place. The Sergeant Pilots had written a song of their own which they called 'Hardships', with the refrain:

'Hardships, yer bastards?

You don't know what hardships are!
Off to Russia we did go,
To this land of ice and snow,
And a glass of Russian tea,
Tasted just like maidens' pee,
Hardships, yer bastards?
You don't know what hardships are!'
(There were, of course, several more verses!)

One particular evening Wag Haw and Ibby Waud, who were the last to leave the Sergeants' Mess, forgot to switch the light off. They were both in a particularly happy and carefree mood and Ibby being adept with a gun took out his revolver and shot the bulb which seemed hilarious! News travelled fast and it wasn't long before the CO Ramsbottom Isherwood got to hear about it and called them in. A short crisp talk about closing down the bar was all that was needed. To be fair they weren't the only two chaps, either in the Sergeants' Mess or of the Officers' Mess to 'burst out' during this waiting period and the CO had to put his foot down occasionally to stop things getting out of hand.

At this time the engineering and wireless units were still hard at work. The engineer officer, Flight Lieutenant Gittins, was holding examinations for Russian technicians, whose results astonished him. Only some weeks previously the Russians had known nothing of the Hurricane and had had to learn engineering and maintenance skills through the medium of an interpreter and yet their average pass mark was in the region of eighty per cent. Gittins said that he had set the examination himself and ensured that there was no easy marking. The only problem he had was because the Russian technicians arrived rather late in the mornings and insisted on carrying on well into the evenings!

Occasionally, when the weather lifted and the light was passable, usually during late morning, the Russians would take off in their Hurricanes. Three squadrons of Soviet pilots could then fly them and had enough experience to teach others. Likewise, Russian ground crews were self-sufficient in servicing and maintaining them. A few pilots including the diminutive figure of Flight Lieutenant Ross from 134 Squadron went down to Flights from day to day to give a hand on matters of instruction.

The Russian pilots were competent, experienced and didn't need a lot of instruction to get to grips with the Hurricane. Squadron Leader Tony Miller of 134 Squadron summed them up when he said, 'All in all, the Russians had one great asset, they had guts.

They thought nothing of the Hun and were quite prepared to take on the Me 109s in their 220-mph biplanes. They would fly in the most awful weather; their bombers were doing three or four sorties a day from Vianga; and eventually they were doing bombing raids with old flying boats fitted with skis. We used to call them the "Russki Walrus" and they had about the same performance and armament.'

As the days were crossed off on the calendar for November there was still nothing positive from the Air Ministry with regard to the evacuation of the Wing. After an interchange of numerous cables London had abandoned the bright idea of transporting the Wing by rail over 2,000 miles through Southern Russia to the Middle East. Nobody had any doubts that the RAF would organize an evacuation and most thought that the Navy would arrive to take them home.

Towards the end of their stay the Royal Navy called into Polyarno, a Russian Naval base, with their submarine HMS *Trident*. The sailors soon found out that there was an RAF contingent in the vicinity and it was arranged that a small representation should visit the Wing. They arrived one afternoon, Officers, Petty Officers and ratings and were soon delegated to their respective Messes. Flight Sergeant Micky Turner remembered that, 'It was like a night out on the town. Those Navy guys had been pent up in their sub for quite a long time and a very relaxed time was had by all, resulting in a lot of horizontal bodies.'

The next morning the submariners took a selection of RAF types back with them for the night and Micky, needless to say, represented the Sergeants. To their surprise the *Trident*, which had been 'Swinging the Compass' turned up at the dockside and took them back to Polyarno on the surface. Then they clambered out and went with the crew to the barracks which had been allotted to them by the Russians. They had a meal and gathered in one room for the rest of the evening. Never in all his life had Micky Turner met a group of people with such a fantastic sense of humour. The antics those submariners got up to that night defied description, he said, singing 'This Ole Shirt of Mine', and trying to get the RAF types to become members of the 'Blue Flame Club'. He laughed so much that he almost 'flaked out'.

The next morning they were roused to a surprise 'wakey wakey' and then they were on their way. The submarine commander decided to take them out to sea and do some exercises with a couple of Russian destroyers. They took it in turns to sit in their quarters, which in turn served as the sleeping quarters, Mess deck and recreation set-up. In the centre of the room above the table was a rack fastened to the ceiling and attached to this rack was an open top can which swung gently backwards and forwards. This pot contained all the knives, forks and spoons for the Mess. As the sub dived it was uncanny to see this mess tin take up an angle of 25–30 degrees to the table and vice-versa. All the time they sat there, the off-duty crew fed them with 'have you heard this one?'

Then the submariners got down to some serious business. They were about 30–35 ft below when the order to surface and man the 4.7 in gun was given. They were undoing the hatch at 10 ft down and then up they went, with the ammunition, going through a hatch in the Pantry. They fired off 4 rounds and were back down to 30 ft in 3 minutes 41 seconds.

A few days later the Wing received a signal that Royal Naval transports would shortly be arriving in Murmansk to take them home. There were farewell parties with Russian friends including one rather large booze-up given by the Wing itself which Flight Lieutenant Griffith recorded in his diary of events:

'The long, echoing, first floor corridor of our Kremlin — the only space in it large enough to accommodate half-a-hundred Russians to whom we had sent written invitations, was laid out to look like a party — with tables stretching down it covered with white table-cloths, extra electric-lights installed for the occasion, some green stuff plucked from neighbouring birch-forests draped round the lamps, and the tables groaning under bottles of English spirits and Russian edibles — an amateurish affair when compared with the hospitality of the Berkeley in London or the Metropole in Moscow — but serving its turn within the frozen rim of the Arctic Circle, and enjoyed by all. As a party — like the small expedition as a whole — it was a classic.'

There was little packing to do except for personal belongings because they had handed over all their gear and equipment to the Russians. There were no letters from home to tuck away because none of them had received any mail for four months. The lack of mail had affected the chaps more than anything else, as Micky Turner put it when looking back over his experiences in Russia:

'The Russian Expedition to me was a challenge — it was something different! Different circumstances, different culture and climate, nothing cut and dried — improvization was rampant and this is something I enjoy — you did your job based on your common sense, mixed with initiative and "know how". The housing was different, food above average, and we mostly made our own entertainment — we also knew that we weren't going to be there forever. Russia wouldn't be the part of the world I would like to live in. Our standards are very much above theirs and it is after all a form of punishment to go without the small but essential things that help to make life worthwhile, especially news from home! Hence, four months was our limit.'

One member of the Expedition had to leave behind a rather special present. The CO, Wing Commander Ramsbottom Isherwood, had been given a baby reindeer by Major General Kuznetsov as a token of their friendship and mutual understanding. This event was mentioned in Daily Routine Orders on 5 November and read as follows; 'A reindeer has been taken on Wing-strength from today's date. Volunteer (preferably with experience) to report to Orderly Room for duties of grooming, feeding and exercising same.'

This was a symbolic gesture on behalf of the Russian General and a sign of their friendship. No man could have done more than Major General Kuznetsov to ensure the success of the Expedition.

Chapter 13
HMS Kenya

The last and largest party comprising 151 Wing embarked at the port of Murmansk on the cruiser HMS *Kenya*. As she cast off early one evening the RAF contingent on board heaved a sigh of relief thinking that at last they were on their way home. Throughout their stay in Russia life had been full of surprises but there was one more in store for them which they hadn't in the least expected. The ship had just got under way when the Convoy Commodore announced over the tannoy that they were going to search for a German convoy which was sneaking up the Norwegian coast. It seemed to some of them that Mother Russia wasn't going to let them go without a struggle!

They were at 'action stations' from the very start of their trip in the calmness of the night and even while admiring the fantastic view of the 'aurora borealis'. It seemed as if these northern lights were right above the cruiser, hanging down like moving multicoloured curtains and illuminating the whole of the deck. There was no sign of the German convoy as the *Kenya* made its way round the Rybachiy Peninsula and across Varanger Fiord. Then the Commodore announced that they were retracing their steps to bombard Vardo, a Norwegian port.

Ibby Waud who was in one of the gun turrets with his back to the steel wall was fascinated watching the Norwegian coastline getting closer and closer as the cruiser edged her way through the calm waters. They got in so close that he could see quite distinctly the headlights of a car winding its way up the mountain road at the back of the harbour. He had never been in a naval action before and hadn't the least idea what to expect. The atmosphere inside the turret was claustrophobic and as they stealthily got closer to the coast he could feel excitement mounting as they waited for the action to come. When his guns opened fire he felt as if he had stuck his head into a volatile thunder and lightning cloud. All hell had suddenly broken loose and at first he thought he had lost his eyesight from the flash of the weapons. His ears had clogged up and he could feel the steel wall of the turret vibrating madly as the cruiser slid backwards in the water from the recoil of the shells.

Down below through holes in the floor of the turret he watched matelots feeding shells onto a conveyor belt carrying them up to the guns and it sickened him to think what might happen to those poor bastards down there in the bowels of the ship if the *Kenya* was to be clobbered. Most of the other RAF types had also been a little shattered during the action. Micky Turner who was standing up on deck said that, 'After a time of recuperation I realized that I could see a little and it got progressively better — my mate underwent the same experience and it wasn't long before we acclimatized ourselves to the perpendicular — in other words only when the ship was vertical did the guns open fire and we closed our eyes!'

After the action which the Navy underplayed as being a small sideshow the Commodore told them over the tannoy that they would be returning to Murmansk for a while before sailing home. This news was naturally disappointing as everyone had been geared up by the thought of going home and tying up in the harbour at Murmansk was rather a let down.

Finally they were really on their way home — in rough seas and battened down for a couple of days — but that didn't matter. During the journey Wag Haw was informed over the ship's radio that he had been awarded the 'Order of Lenin' as the top-scoring fighter pilot of 151 Wing. The CO, Ramsbottom Isherwood, and both Squadron commanders, Tony Rook and Tony Miller also received the Order.

There was naturally a general air of excitement aboard when HMS *Kenya* finally docked at Rosyth in Scotland on 7 December. The prospect of going on leave after having 'done their stuff' in Russia made them feel keyed up and anxious to get home. Then came the momentous news over the radio that evening that Japan had just attacked Pearl harbor, which they knew was bound to bring the Yanks into the war. They were pleased and relieved to hear that America had at last been drawn into the action and most of them thought that the war had reached a turning point.

*   *   *

151 Wing was disbanded upon its return to the UK and all members sent off on leave. But for those pilots, headquarters and ground staff the Russian adventure had been merely an interlude in the pursuit of a long war. After a few days' leave they received new postings — most in rather more congenial surroundings than those in the Artic Circle!

Members of the Expedition were surprised to find that their activities in Russia had generated a great deal of national, regional and local publicity up and down the country. The Russians had sent photographs and film material to the Air Ministry for distribution to press and cinema news networks who were only too eager to report on the 'RAF in Russia'. Various members of the Expedition, while on leave, found reporters on their doorstep waiting to interview their local hero and most nationals from *The Times* to the *Daily Mirror* took up the story.

During the war the Press had to get clearance to print any story of this nature but there were many good reasons why both the Air Ministry and the Ministry of Information had sent out official releases and allowed individual members to be interviewed. The Ministries had seized on the opportunity of using the success of the RAF Expedition to Russia as a major propaganda exercise on the domestic front.

Premier Stalin had been demanding the impossible in late 1941 by calling on Britain to invade Europe but by the end of the year the Russians had admitted casualties of over four million which indicates how dire the situation was. Communists in Britain had begun daubing walls with 'Second Front Now' and agitators were causing trouble in war factories. The massive aid programme for Russia was just getting under way and although details of British intent in this respect had been published in the more serious newspapers the public at large were still ignorant of what was really going on. Something was needed to capture their imagination in an emotional sense.

The concept of the Expedition and the achievements of the fighter squadrons provided an excellent platform for a publicity exercise. Wag Haw and his girlfriend, May, for example, found themselves on the front pages of the national press. Even his local newspaper urged readers to come and see him in action on the Russian front in British Movietone News at the Embassy cinema. His father received letters of congratulation on his son becoming a 'Hero of the Soviet Union' from factory workers and union officials in surrounding areas. To further the propaganda campaign generated by the press, radio and cinema, Wag and some of the other pilots were sent on visits to factories making tanks and guns for Russia.

151 Wing also received coverage in Russian newspapers and on cinema screens. Usually British pilots and technicians were featured in company with their Russian counterparts as part of a theme 'fighting the common enemy'. It was quite amazing that the Russians should have photographed and taken film of events at Vianga when the country was struggling desperately for survival. Their war was on such a gigantic scale that it was equally surprising that the progress of a small RAF Wing on the remote Northern Russian front should have been brought to the attention of the Russian public.

The award of four 'Orders of Lenin' to members of the Wing by the Russian High Command ensured its place in Russian military history. They were the only ones to be given to Allied Forces during the whole of the Second World War which indicates the importance of this Expedition in the eyes of the Russians. On the other hand it seems rather strange that those RAF men who went to Russia did not receive even a British campaign medal and that the story of the Expedition rated only a bare mention in RAF history. The squadron badges of Nos 81 and 134 were embellished to commemorate the Squadrons' activities in Russia, number 81 Squadron having a red star in the centre and 134's central gauntlet coloured in red.

*   *   *

The impact of this small Expedition both at home and in Russia was quite extraordinary. Upon embarkation the Wing had made a valuable contribution to Anglo/Russian mutual cooperation during 1941 — the critical period of the Second World War: a time when Russia had only been our ally for a matter of weeks and with whom collaboration was extremely difficult. It is only when people get together that they can develop understanding and mutual respect for one another and the Expedition achieved this in the wild tundra wastes of Northern Russia. This book, therefore, is essentially a human story concerning the coming together of two vastly different peoples against a background of a momentous and savage war.

In the finale of his diary Hubert Griffith emphasized that despite the fact that in the winter of 1941 the Russians looked like losing the war they had supreme confidence in themselves, their resources and in Mother Russia. He went on to give two instances which illustrated their character and ruthless determination. Late one night he was walking back along the snow-covered road from the village to the camp having despaired of the local cinema show. The stars were out and moonlight cast a ghostly beam across the lonely countryside, so that it looked like an empty, frozen Sahara desert. In the shadows of a hillside he was passed by a convoy of lorries carrying Russian soldiers who were singing in chorus, loudly and cheerfully and apparently without a care in the world. He knew that they were not putting on an act for his benefit because nobody could see him and he could hear their voices fading away in the distance. There had been no doubt in his mind that night that the average Russian soldier in those parts was content with his lot and happy to be doing what he did.

The second instance concerned a Russian pilot who had been entertained in the Mess and had become a particular friend. This chap had had a scrap over the lines with two German aircraft and after shooting down one he rammed the second and then baled out. By the merest fluke he landed close to two Germans who had force landed out there in the tundra. Griffith said, 'the Russian pilot fought them on foot. He shot one with his revolver, and then shot the Boxer dog that the German pilot had, for some reason, brought with him. He then had a hand-to-hand grapple with the second German — having a few teeth knocked out and his face slashed from forehead to chin in the process — before killing the second German by firing his Very cartridge pistol into him at close range. The Russian then walked back for four days through the snow with his feet frostbitten and retired to sick quarters.' The RAF medical officer visited the Russian in hospital and confirmed the medical details of this remarkable achievement. This incident, as Griffith said, typified the spirit in which the Russians were fighting the war.

The Russians for their part had had a unique opportunity of working alongside an Allied Air Force. Not one Russian bomber had been lost when escorted by RAF fighters and fifteen German aircraft had been shot down for the loss of one British Hurricane pilot, which, by any standard, is an impressive record. The Soviets had also been able to discuss combat tactics and formation techniques with their British counterparts and received instruction in the art of flying and servicing the Hurricane. As the British were going home the Russian authorities had one simple message for them, 'Send us more Hurricanes', they said.

Britain and America sent over 14,000 aircraft (including thousands of Hurricanes) to Russia throughout the course of the war as part of a vast military aid programme. The Expedition, therefore, was not merely a symbolic gesture to 'wave the flag' but it paved the way for the enormous 'back up' of supplies some of which were in the pipeline when 151 Wing arrived on the scene. It was an advance party of considerable importance in that it had to achieve a high standard of performance and behave in an exemplary fashion — which it did throughout.

For most of those who went on the Expedition the Russian interlude was the greatest adventure of their lives. It is now 46 years since it happened and perhaps this book will reawaken memories of survivors and give 151 Wing its rightful place in RAF history. There are many forgotten stories about RAF exploits which have gradually surfaced over the years but this one must be unique.

One of the pilots on 134 Squadron was Pilot Officer Neil (Jock) Cameron who later became Marshal of the Royal Air Force. He wrote to his friend Micky Turner in 1973 saying that it would be difficult to forget those days in Russia. 'I thought we had a good bunch of characters,' he said 'and if I find time I shall do a book on the RAF in Russia.' Unfortunately Sir Neil died before he was able to do so, but I hope that this work will serve as a tribute to the men of the 151 Wing, their exemplary record in Russia and their unique contribution to the war effort.

Aftermath

Following the Russian Expedition both Wag Haw and his great friend Ibby Waud were to realize their boyhood dreams of becoming fighter aces. Wag became a Wing Commander and by the end of the war was leading a Wing of long-range Mustangs having been awarded the DFC, DFM and Order of Lenin. Ibby stayed with 81 Squadron and went to the Middle East winning a DFC and Croix de Guerre. He served with 81 Squadron for two-and-a-half years, rising from Sergeant Pilot to senior Flight commander.

The Russians have never allowed Wag Haw to forget that he is a 'Hero of the Soviet Union' and over the years he has been their guest at special functions both in London and Moscow. Last year, for example, he was in Moscow to be presented with a Gold Medal commemorating the fortieth anniversary of the ending of the war in Europe. He told the author then that whenever he goes to Russia he is accorded the style and privileges of the VIP and is never allowed to spend money of his own.

Shortly after Wag's Moscow trip Ibby Waud and Ginger Carter, both from 81 Squadron, were presented with anniversary gold medals at the Russian Embassy in London. The author attended the ceremony and later had a meeting with the then Russian Ambassador, His Excellency Victor Popov, who expressed great interest in the book and arranged meetings with Russian officials. Vladimir Ivanov, editor of *Soviet Weekly*, *Soviet News* and chief representative of the Novosti Press Agency, provided a mass of background material and photographs from the archives.

When researching this material it was surprising to find recent articles featuring 151 Wing's activities, after all the years. The entire back page of the 26 January 1985 edition of *Soviet Weekly*, for example, was a pictorial feature of the Wing spotlighting Wag Haw as 'The Hero of Murmansk'. In sharp contrast, serving as a reminder of the climate in that part of the world was a short piece on the front page entitled, 'Coldest winter hits Murmansk'. This went on to report:

'The people of Murmansk, in the Soviet Far North, went without gas cookers for five days this month when city authorities cut off the mains for fear of the gas liquefying in the coldest winter on record. Milk bottles exploded spontaneously in the cold and on January the 5th the temperature in the city plunged to –47 degrees C.'

This story of the 'Hurricanes over Murmansk' owes a great deal to Hubert Griffith, the Wing Adjutant, who painstakingly kept a diary of events recording the history of 151 Wing. His excellent slim little volume entitled, *RAF in Russia* which appeared in March 1942 was kindly loaned by Wing Commander A. J. McGregor DSO who was a Flying Officer serving with 81 Squadron. The author has endeavoured to contact Mr Griffith and his publisher without success, but 46 years is a long time. Hubert Griffith obviously had a great enthusiasm for life and with his knowledge of Russia a sincere desire to get on with her people. This was reflected in his diary and his words have been quoted wherever possible because they were written on the spot during those traumatic times.

The author particularly wishes to thank Wag Haw and Ibby Waud for all their cooperation. They are still a great team and to hear Wag on the piano with both of them singing,

'Hardships, yer bastards?
Yer don't know what hardships are!'

brings one right into the atmosphere of the Sergeants' Mess at Vianga.

Fighter pilots A. J. McGregor and Ginger Carter were of great help. Also Micky Turner, the engineer, who came over from Canada with so much 'gen'. Doctor John Fenton who sailed into Archangel in convoy 'PQ3' provided a lot of background regarding that terrible winter of 1941. And the former RAF test pilot John Gibson AFC, who had completed an Arctic Indoctrination Course, was a mine of information on all matters concerning climate and aeroplanes of those times.

Recently on the TV 'Mastermind' programme an expert who had selected RAF History throughout World War Two as a subject was asked the name of an RAF aircraft which had seen action in Russia and failed to answer. Perhaps this book will now fill the gap on the subject!

Bibliography

Hitler's War on Russia by Paul Carell, George G. Harrap.

The Right of the Line by John Terraine, Hodder and Stoughton.

Winston S. Churchill (Volume V1), by Martin Gilbert, Heinemann.

Marshal of the Soviet Union G. Zhukov (Volume 1) by G. Zhukov, Progress Publishers, Moscow.

Horrido! by Trevor J. Constable and Colonel Raymond F. Toliver, published by Arthur Barker.

General Chernyakhovsky by A. Sharipov, Progress Publishers, Moscow.

RAF in Russia by Hubert Griffith, Hammond, Hammond and Company.

The Luftwaffe — A History by John Killen, Frederick Muller.

Fighter Squadrons of the RAF by John Rawlings, Macdonald, London.

The Battle of Britain by Len Deighton, Jonathan Cape.

Of further interest . . .

THE DAY OF THE TYPHOON
Flying with the RAF tankbusters in Normandy

John Golley

Moving inexorably towards the danger mark, the needle of the radiator temperature gauge only bore out what Bob Stanford already feared — that his engine, hit by enemy flak, was on the point of blowing up and that he would either have to bale out or attempt to crash-land. That the latter option was the wrong choice seemed to be confirmed within seconds as a limping Spitfire, clearly in trouble, crossed the nose of the earthward-plunging Typhoon, obviously intent on putting down in the same battle-scarred field. Suddenly transformed from aerial avengers to sitting ducks, both pilots found themselves on the ground and running for cover under the protection of a brandy-toting Company Sergeant Major.

Fast paced, and reading more like fiction than fact, this fascinating picture of six weeks in the life of a rocket Typhoon squadron is an authentic portrayal of the machines and the pilots whose skill and daring in close ground-support operations helped to make the Invasion of Europe a success.

'. . . uniquely successful in recreating the atmosphere of crew-room life, and the split-second reactions of combat . . .' — Wing Commander Roland Beamont CBE, DSO and Bar, DFC and Bar, FRAeS.